W0254126

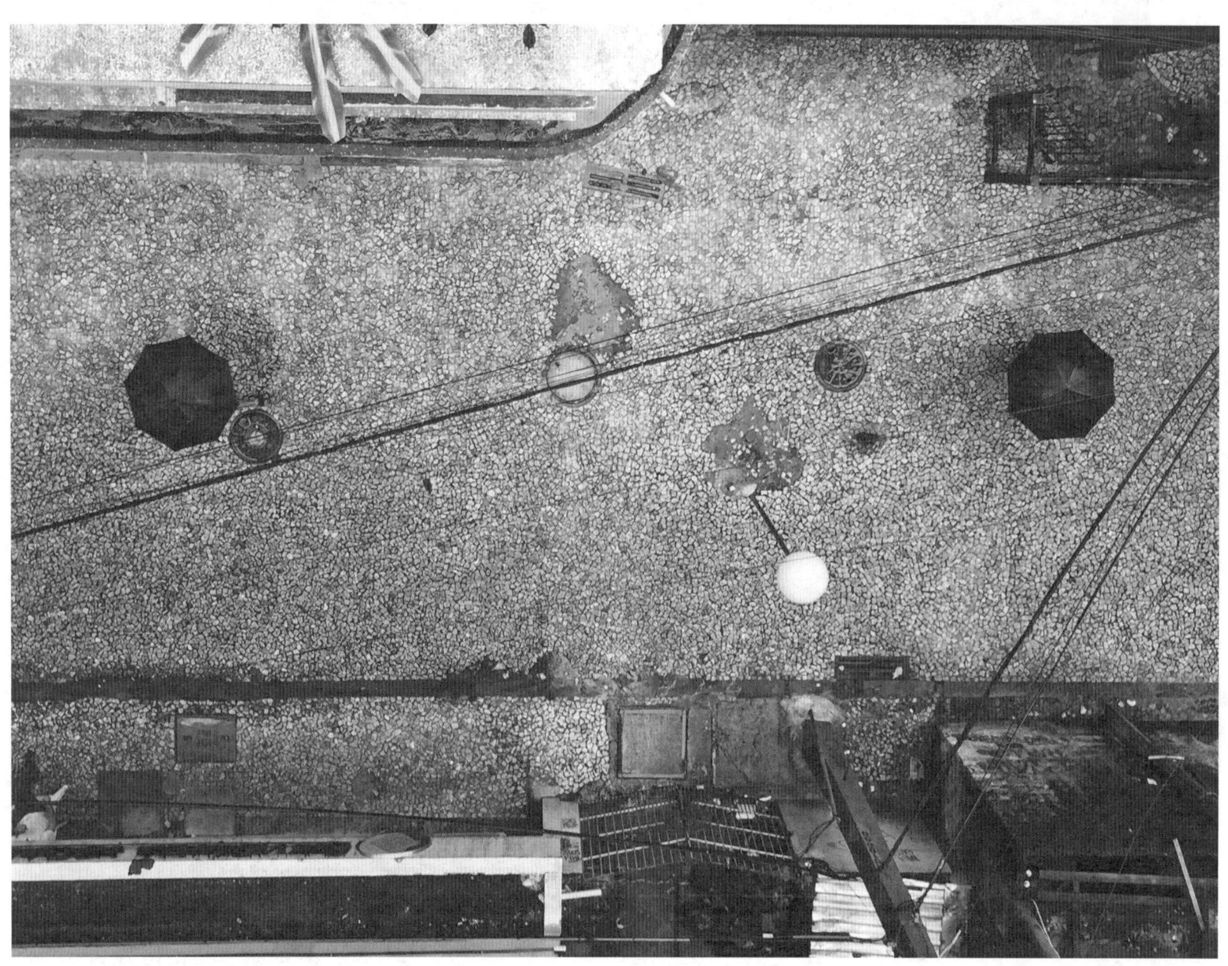

JEREMY GLAHOLT
PERNAMBUCO, 2015

LOS ANGELES REVIEW OF BOOKS QUARTERLY JOURNAL | SUMMER 2015

COVER ART
CLARISSA TOSSIN
WHEN TWO PLACES LOOK ALIKE, 2012-2013
DIGITAL CHROMOGENIC PRINTS, 40 X 27"

The Los Angeles Review of Books is a 501(c)(3) nonprofit organization. The *LARB Quarterly Journal* is published quarterly by the Los Angeles Review of Books, 1614 S. Central Ave., Glendale, CA 91204. Printed in Los Angeles. Submissions for the *Journal* can be emailed to EDITORIAL@LAREVIEWOFBOOKS.ORG. Visit our website at WWW.LAREVIEWOFBOOKS.ORG.

The *LARB Quarterly Journal* is a premium of the LARB Membership Program. Annual subscriptions are available. Go to WWW.LAREVIEWOFBOOKS.ORG/MEMBERSHIP for more information or email MEMBERSHIP@LAREVIEWOFBOOKS.ORG.

Distribution through Publishers Group West. If you are a retailer and would like to order the *LARB Quarterly Journal*, call 800-788-3123 or email orderentry@perseusbooks.com.

To place an ad in the *LARB Quarterly Journal*, email ADSALES@LAREVIEWOFBOOKS.ORG.

ZACH HARRIS
LINEN LAST JUDGMENT, 2014–2015
WATER BASED PAINT, INK, LINEN, WOOD
72 X 54 1/2 X 7/8"
COURTESY OF THE ARTIST, DAVID KORDANSKY GALLERY, FEUER/MESLER GALLERY

ALEX OLSON
ARTICULATION, 2009
OIL ON LINEN
COURTESY OF LAURA BARTLETT GALLERY, LONDON AND SHANE CAMPELL GALLERY, CHICAGO

HOMELAND INSECURITY

MARY KAY ZURAVLEFF

EACH MORNING, I'd climb down the ladder from the top bunk to my bedroom floor, landing as lightly as I could. It was impossible to predict what might set my father off — just taking a shower could crack the day wide open. What if you forgot to turn the bathroom fan on, allowing the mirror to fog up? Or you forgot to turn the fan *off*, not only a waste of electricity but also a potential fire hazard? What if you left hair in the drain or a wet towel on the floor? Honestly, you could get in trouble with him six ways before breakfast. After the yelling stopped, there might be an hour or a week of silence aimed your way.

If, against your family's wishes, you become a writer, it is your job to trace those eggs back to the coop, in this case back to an Old Believers community in Erie, Pennsylvania. In a house above the train tracks, where the lake breezes carried the stench of the paper mills, there lived 11 children whose illiterate father worked in a factory and whose mother, though born here, lost her US citizenship when she married a Russian national — that's how it was in 1908. My grandmother was 14 years old when she did that, and, beginning at 15, she had a child nearly every two years, except for the year she had identical twin girls.

My father was born in 1931, the last of the 11 children. He used to say his parents were too poor to give them middle names. The rare childhood stories he tells are of his father whipping him with a leather strap made for that purpose, like the time he hit his next older brother right between the eyes with a dart. But he also remembers ice-skating on Lake Erie while his father fished beneath the lake's frozen crust; the pike stiffened as my grandfather laid them on the ice. At home, the fish swam again in a barrel of water in the basement. My grandfather would crack the film of ice on the water and grab one when my grandmother wanted fresh fish to fry. My father attended a technical high school, "for hoodlums," one relative told me, so he'd have a trade. But he also ended up going to Princeton because of his astonishing basketball talent and raw intelligence.

Years later, when my father offered his parents a trip to Russia, my grandfather said, "Why would I want to go there? I fled from Russia." He actually said that in Russian, because he stopped speaking English after he retired. He also grew a long beard and spent more time at the Orthodox Church, modeled on the one back in Russia. There, bearded men in Russian shirts prayed on one side, and women in headscarves and floor-length skirts prayed on the other. Except for time spent bowing, the congregation stood through all the services, which were chanted in Slavonic. They were keeping the faith, and by faith I mean the Old Believers version of Orthodoxy that had been run out of Russia centuries earlier.

My mother's ancestors fled from the same rural village as my father's; born a coal miner's daughter in West Virginia, my mom grew up in Erie, four blocks from my dad. Her people loved history and storytelling, until you asked about the Old Country. "What's to know?" my Great-Aunt Pearl would say. "They drank too much and beat their wives." By then, Pearl had become a Presbyterian; however, the rest of both families remained Orthodox, which forbids its followers from marrying outside the faith. Once when I asked my mother what drew her to my father, she said, "There weren't many choices — he was the best of the lot."

After my siblings' births and before mine, General Electric transferred my parents away from Erie, though we came back for weddings, funerals, Easter, and two weeks every other summer. Between them, my parents had eight siblings and all four of their parents in that town. No matter how many picnics, dinners, or brunches we attended during our summer "vacations," one or more of my aunts would invariably be mad at us. Mom said their feelings were hurt; having grown up with nothing, they wanted to cook a feast for their baby brother and show him the home they'd made for themselves. There weren't enough days to go around, yet they expected us for dinner. They also expected us at church.

My mom's mother always managed to have long bibbed skirts in my sister's and my sizes, as well as a Russian shirt for my brother. (She kept spare blouses and headscarves in the closet on her "burial clothes" shelf.) With our parents, we'd walk four blocks from my mother's parents' house to my father's parents' — passing three aunts' and uncles' houses along the way — and then turn the corner to the gold-domed Church of the Nativity. Inside the door stood a scowling woman, presumably the greeter, who would gesture toward a stack of quilted prayer squares; you were supposed to bring one in and toss it on the wooden floor in front of where you stood. When you bowed to the floor, the square was for cushioning your head. Rather than take the top square, I would take the time to select one of the patterns. The scowling woman did not approve.

No matter when we got to church, a service was already underway. We would enter the dark sanctuary as the wizard-robed and bearded priest was swinging around a censer, whose musty frankincense my mother and I despised. If my mom's father was there, I'd hear his coughing on the other side of the sanctuary: the poor man had black lung from his years in the coal mines, and he worked as a bartender at the Russian Club; the last thing he needed was to have smoke waved in his face.

My sister and I flanked my mother and followed her lead: when she crossed herself three times and bowed, touching her forehead to the ground, we did too. It was like the head-shoulders-knees-and-toes routine of gym class, which I performed haphazardly. In my mother's time, if any scowling crabapple-faced women saw her cross herself sloppily or skip a bow, they would flick her on the head, the same way they'd flick a fly off the braided bread at a church supper.

I listened to the priest chant as well as to the choir members, most of whom were my cousins, but the endless service was more foreign than familial, more spooky than spiritual. To distract myself from wanting to sit down, I watched two boys on library ladders light row after row of icons, ribbons of smoke from the olive oil lamps and beeswax candles wafting through the church. When all the wicks in front of all the icons were lit, the boys snuffed them out one by one.

Filing out of the church, the scowling women smiled and hugged me, mostly because they recognized my mother in me, and then we went to an aunt's house for blintzes and *studzienina*, a dish of jellied pigs' feet, which they knew was my father's favorite. He always remarked on whatever his sisters had added to the mix — chunks of chicken and veal that had been far beyond their reach during the Depression. He said it tasted different because of these luxuries and that he missed the stripped-down version. We never developed a taste for the dish. Being starving is the only reason I can see for eating a jiggly dish of pigs' feet; my father sucked the knuckle bones for scraps of meat.

My parents and their families battled poverty and prejudice in the New Country. Our biggest hurdle growing up was avoiding our father's baffling rage. It's possible that a strong extended family and a strict religion kept their generation from going under. Microloans are all the rage now, but my mother has abundant stories of how a little help from family or church changed someone's fate; a $100 gift spared her own parents from the coal mines and bankrolled their move to Erie. They, in turn, were always helping someone get back on their feet or get a fresh start.

Neither of my parents speak much Russian, though they can understand some. (My dad talked to his father in English, and his father answered in Russian.) Their generation was in a tug-of-war between assimilation and faith. My mother wondered if leaving Erie had left my father at loose ends, which is not precisely how he seemed. Released from that tug-of-war, another man might have relaxed, but this guy was tied up in knots. Going back there wound him up tighter, making family vacations especially dicey. For road trips, you were to get yourself and your packed duffel in the car, or the car would leave without you. If you forgot, you improvised, and that included toothbrush or underwear, because we would not be wasting time or money when we had toothbrushes and underwear at home.

Now, I live in Washington, DC, and my parents are in Oklahoma City, where General Electric eventually moved us. My family's unusual religious background occasionally comes up at dinner parties, though the Old Believers of the Russian Orthodox Church can be a conversation-stopper. Most of my parents' generation has died, and we were never in Erie long enough to bond with our cousins, partly because we ate with a different group of them every night, once every two years. I married a kind, flexible man, whose generosity toward our children continues to impress all of us, and we have raised two children with no religious affiliation. Meanwhile, I'm still walking on eggs. Once, when my husband innocently asked me, "How old are you?," I instinctively replied, "What did I do?" He was as surprised as I was, maybe more so, because I realized why I'd jumped. "How old are you?" was one of the questions my father asked before he started yelling — whatever your age, you were old enough to know better.

It is old news that our childhood hard-wires us. Now, geneticists and neuroscientists are busy discovering that our very circuit boards have been generations in the making. Like a propensity for breast cancer or sickle-cell anemia, we may be genetically predisposed to suffering and paranoia, to storytelling and engineering.

I write all this to explain my panic when, two summers ago, my husband suggested adding another destination to our vacation. After visiting our son in Copenhagen, he proposed, we should take our daughter and go to Russia. No, I said. No, that's not a good idea. Our son, who speaks Russian, wouldn't be able to come with us. My husband knew that. He was lobbying for us to spend a few days in St. Petersburg, where we could get by speaking English. We'd be there during July's White Nights, and we could enjoy the Hermitage, palaces, ballet, churches, and borscht in Peter the Great's capital city. I pointed out that Peter the Great tortured and drove out the Russian Orthodox priests before he tortured and then killed his own son. My husband suggested that what happened in the 18th century stayed in the 18th century. An avid genealogist, he asked me, "Don't you want to see your homeland?"

Frankly, I was afraid of my homeland. I was afraid that some capricious authoritarian would not let me in, or that another would not let me out. I was sure there would be impenetrable rules governing food, clothing, and behavior, and I would be found wanting. I would get in trouble or lost, and not speaking the language, I would not be able to get help. Or a toothbrush or underwear, should I forget to pack them. Russia was a family trip back to the ground zero of family.

Speaking of family, around this time things had become tenser than usual in my family of origin: my brother had announced he was divorcing himself from my parents. Devastated, my mother claimed to be blindsided by his version of our childhood, and my sister, who rightly pointed out that our stroke-addled father could no longer harm us, wanted my brother to get over it already. I was talking to all of them and reeling with their pain even as my sympathetic husband was making ready to get me out of the country.

When we told our daughter, gently, our tentative plans, she said, "St. Petersburg? Cool beans." That was my first indication that I was overreacting. We told my mother, expecting her usual refrain, "Those people love to suffer." Instead, she said, "I am so jealous. I have always wanted to see St. Petersburg." I had not seen that coming, but I should have. She and my father still said their prayers in Slavonic every night, and she had a firm grip on church history, from its early break from the Catholic Church to the stubborn separatism of the Old Believers. We offered to take her, but she didn't think she could manage.

I have to admit that I was still afraid when I submitted the visa information, lest I unwittingly commit some kind of perjury, and I was afraid handing over my passport, lest the visa office not return it. On one level, I knew their harshest punishment would be to make me resubmit the forms until I got them right, but my heart beat in my throat at every step.

In Copenhagen, we rode through the canals and climbed the city's towers, joined by our son and his resourceful girlfriend, who was working on a farm outside the city. My kind of vacation — good company, castles, and chocolate — but my anxiety returned when we boarded the plane for Russia. For one thing, how unhappy all the passengers looked, even the stiletto-heeled, leather-skirted women. Upon landing, the St. Petersburg airport appeared to be boarded up; in fact, it was a crowded and confused construction sight. People quickly abandoned the concept of waiting in line. Here was the very mob scene I'd feared, and I held tight to my daughter's sleeve. "Mom," she assured me, "no one's going to get left behind." It was not lost on me that I should have been reassuring her. The three of us eventually got through customs, and our prearranged driver was waiting to take us to our hotel. As soon as we checked in, our daughter volunteered to lock our passports in the room safe, which would ease one of my worries. The instructions, however, were in a rough approximation of English, and she ended up closing the "personal mini-vault" without "submitting to enter a password"; consequently, our passports were secure but irretrievable. I bravely returned to the lobby and confessed our error, prepared to take a bullet for the family. But the stern desk clerk actually smiled. "You are not the first," he said.

His understanding gave me courage, and our family of three headed into the city, sounding out the Cyrillic to find a restaurant, the Bronze Horseman, and we even found Band-Aids, which we'd forgotten to pack. In the elaborate genealogies we were learning, my daughter kept track of the tsars, tsarinas, and their little tsardines, as we called them. She also proved to be such a navigation whiz that we took our marching orders from her. Our weeklong adventure was a joy, though Russian history was not. Rich and poor, families had huge broods, but few babies lived past the age of three, giving me my first inkling of why a parent might have avoided bonding with his children.

Among the peasants (my people), subjugation and deprivation were a way of life. You could imagine why the youngest of 11 children would bristle when his kid said, "It's not my turn to empty the dishwasher." You could even imagine (without condoning) that a patriarch, terrified that his flock of children might bring disfavor or starvation on the family, might harshly punish rather than patiently point out a misstep.

Royals did not fare much better. "Peter the Great believed his son was a threat, and he had him killed," our guide, Olga, reminded us at Peterhof Palace. "Or he choked on a chicken bone, you never know." Then she pointed out his engineering marvels, which enabled the elaborate fountains to run on gravity alone, and the practical jokes he devised to soak his guests at royal balls. Also, he built St. Petersburg on the backs of his people: an estimated 100,000 serfs and slave laborers died constructing the city. Olga said all this matter-of-factly. Her crazy-making line about Ivan the Terrible, which we heard from others as well, was that he was devastated when "he accidentally killed his son while beating him."

Meanwhile, the more living Russians we saw, the more my husband and I kept remarking that all the men looked like my father. It was unnerving outside the Hermitage to see him standing on a corner or next to his car scanning the street; he'd have one hand in his pocket fingering coins and the other holding a toothpick to his teeth. My dad had never set foot in this country, and yet his posture and mannerisms were everywhere. How much of who we are is where we come from?

Within the Hermitage, the treasures were truly beyond compare; a few years into her reign, Catherine the Great began acquiring paintings by Rembrandt and Raphael, da Vinci and van Dyck, and her successors followed suit; even after the revolution, the museum added roomfuls of Matisses and Picassos. There were also court portraits and entire wings where royals carried on their private lives there in the Winter Palace along the River Neva. We saw so much significant art for the first time, and at the end of the day what our daughter said was, "Catherine the Great learned from Peter to keep her son insecure." We asked her where she'd read that, and she said, "I figured it out." Smart kid, not such a smart policy. A better plan would be to groom the next generation to carry on. Educate them and fill them with confidence, why don't you, rather than assuming they're out to undermine you (or distinguish themselves) and having them beaten or exiled. Unlike Peter the Great, Catherine's son actually lived to succeed her, though he was attacked and killed shortly into his reign. In fact, most of the tsars were assassinated. Considering that the tsar also appointed the patriarch of the church meant that centuries of ruling families exercised their power over not only the people but also their very souls.

And yet it was in the Church of the Savior on Spilled Blood, built atop the site of Alexander II's assassination, where I stopped feeling so oppressed. After many attempts, terrorists succeeded in murdering the reformer Alexander II — a bomb flung into his carriage knocked the tsar into the street, where he was killed by another bomb. His son and successor, who overturned his father's reforms, built a monument to his memory, a church atop the cobblestones still stained with his father's spilled blood. The central tower is 81 meters tall to mark the year of Alexander's death in 1881, and the enameled domes are more Disney than godly.

As churches go, this one isn't that old, and yet it was essentially built twice. Completed in 1907, the church was ransacked in the revolution; it served as a morgue during the Siege and as a warehouse after, when it was called Church of the Savior on Potatoes. In between, it was slated for demolition but the explosives were needed in the war effort. It wasn't until 1970 that restoration began, and it was reopened in 1997.

That's what I knew as we entered the gates. I'd read that the church contains the largest array of mosaics on earth, but I was unprepared for the millions of glass tessarae, gold sandwiched between the layers, which cover the walls, all the way to the ceilings and the domes' interiors. Passing exquisitely rendered images of the worst thuggery and marvelous beneficence, interspersed with motifs from Russian folk art, I begin crying. Tiny glass shards depict Jesus being tortured and killed, miracles as well as the martyred apostles, and Russia's brutalized saints, surrounded by angels, angels, angels. All of which I'd seen on the walls of my parents' church, as wick after wick was lighted in front of enameled icons.

Here, floor to ceiling in golden mosaics, was the story of the last 2,000 years, no gory detail spared. Jesus reviving a decomposing Lazarus, followed by his torture and bloody crucifixion, the lives of the saints in all their gruesome martyrdom, skin flayed or nailed upside down to a cross. That such cruelty and artistry exist side by side frees up something inside me, and I see — through heavy tears — that they have let me in and that they will not keep me. That everyone in my own sweet family is essential, and that no one will be left behind. That I will walk through this graphic novel of a church, and I will walk out the back door with my chosen husband and our beloved daughter. That we will take care of each other.

Here is the vacation I never expected, one where I could leave some baggage behind.

Just as in America, one exits the Church on Spilled Blood through the gift shop. I buy my mother and myself each an enameled Russian egg to dangle from a thin chain around our necks, and my father a T-shirt of the Romanov dynasty, which it turns out he loves.

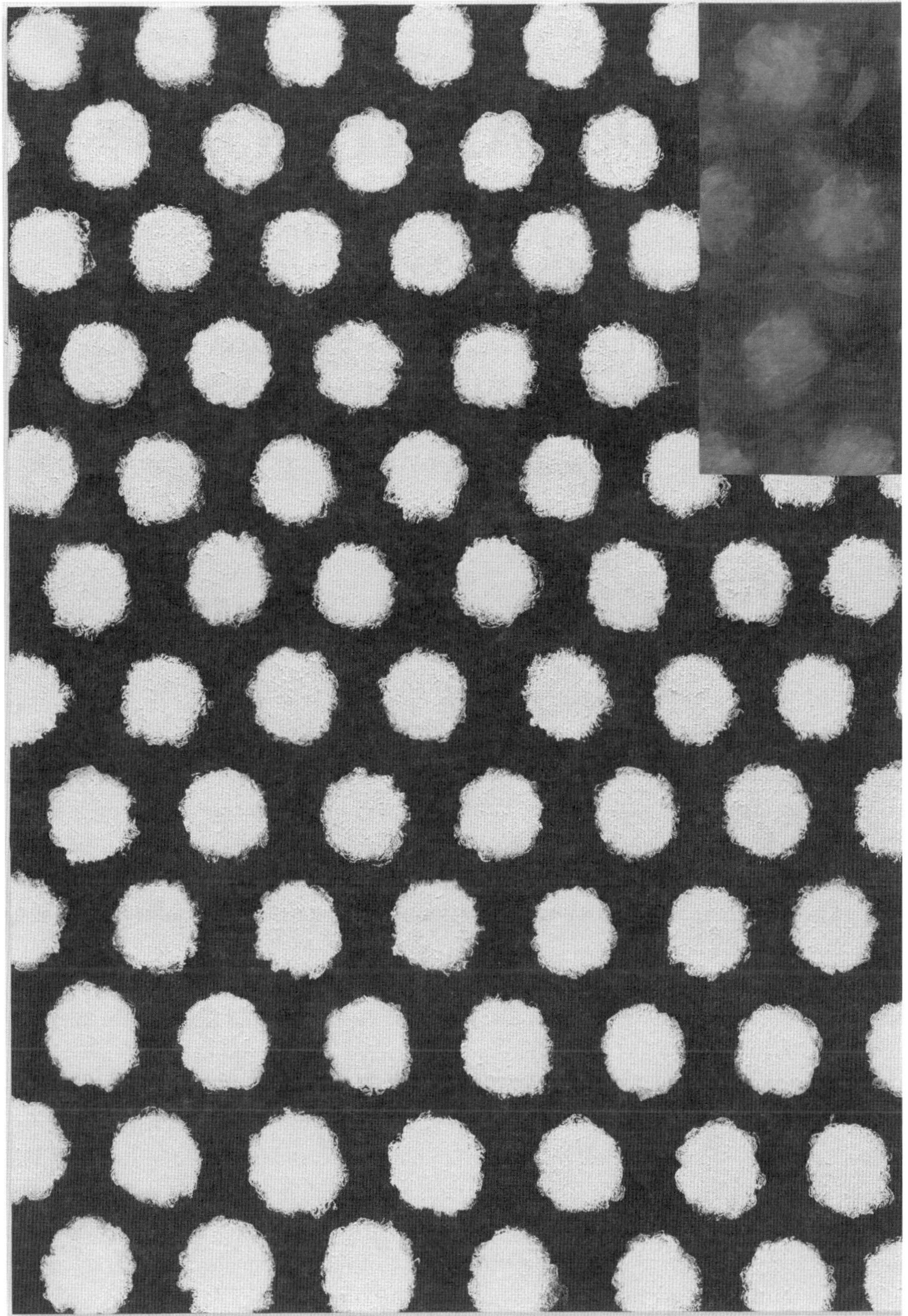

ALEX OLSON
PROPOSAL 14, 2013
OIL ON LINEN
61 X 43 X 3/4"
COURTESY LAURA BARTLETT GALLERY, LONDON

INWARD ASTRONOMY:
ON KNUT HAMSUN'S *HUNGER*, RICK ALVERSON'S *THE COMEDY*, AND MY BRIEF AND WONDROUSLY LONELY LIFE IN OSLO

GAVIN TOMSON

WHEN I WAS 22 YEARS OLD, I did a stupid thing, or maybe it was a smart thing, or maybe both — hopefully it was both. I decided to move from Montreal, where I'd just finished my undergrad and had many friends, to Oslo, where I'd never been and had zero friends, because of a book. This book was *Hunger* (1890), a novel by Knut Hamsun, who won the Nobel Prize for Literature in 1920 and whom James Wood deems "the greatest Norwegian writer since Ibsen." I first read *Hunger* when I was 19, during my freshman year, and yes, the novel changed me. Freud says that the books we read during our adolescence have an extraordinary influence on our lives, that they help us distance ourselves from our parents' ideals and help us form our own ego ideals in their place. *Hunger* influenced me before I even *opened* it. I found it in a used bookstore near campus and the old, yellow-paged text with black and green typography seemed to pull at me, like sleep, and promise a transformative dream. I bought the book for $5.95.

I might as well say it: my initial encounter with *Hunger* was mystical. Mircea Eliade, the Romanian philosopher who wrote *The Sacred and The Profane*, would say that for me *Hunger* functioned as a "hierophany": a "manifestation of the sacred in some ordinary object."

Falling for the first time for a hierophany was much like falling for the first time for a person. In both cases, I wasn't prepared. My confused adolescent self wrote a note in black pen on page v of my copy of *Hunger* (published in 1967 by The Noonday Press and translated by Robert Bly). The note reads, "STARVING ARTIST." There's another note beneath it, "Do your thesis on Nietzsche." This, evidently, is the type of dweeb that I was when I first read *Hunger*, at my poet-friend (and soon-to-be PhD student) Ari's cramped apartment near campus (it smelled of vegetable soup).

"Do you think I'll regret making these notes in pen?" I remember asking Ari.

"Yes," Ari said.

I was stoned.

In 1888, Hamsun anonymously published one part of the four-part *Hunger* in a Dano-Norwegian journal called *Ny Jord* (*New World*). Two years later, he published the complete manuscript, entitled *Sult* (Norwegian for *Hunger*), in Oslo, and afterward he rose to prominence in Scandinavia and elsewhere, particularly Germany. *Hunger* is at once playful and moody and frightening and funny. It's narrated from the highly unreliable, somewhat stream-of-consciousness first-person perspective of a young and starving unnamed writer, eccentric and unhinged and impulsive, based on Hamsun's younger self. The narrator desires only to become a successful writer, but he struggles to publish his work (sound familiar, Dad?). He's caught in a particularly purgatorial catch-22: to eat, he must publish a coherent article, yet to write a coherent article, he must eat. The narrator doesn't care about his physical or mental health; he is starving, but would rather starve than work another job (sound familiar, Dad?). He cares even less about others; he lies to and manipulates them. The reader never learns where the narrator comes from, or if he has any real friends or a family. The narrator is unknowable.

The narrator is also unpredictable. He himself doesn't know what he'll do from one instant to the next. In many ways he's enviously at home in the present. James Wood notes in his essay on *Hunger* in the *London Review of Books* that Hamsun "took from Dostoevsky the idea that plot is not something that merely happens to a character, but that a really strange character leads plot around like an obedient dog." The narrator of *Hunger* is so strange that some critics, including Wood (this time in his book *How Fiction Works*), deem him "insane." Perhaps he is insane or perhaps he isn't — or perhaps, I wonder, is it beside the point? The narrator of *Hunger* is not, of course, a person; he's a narrator. (In Wood's words, Hamsun's narrators and characters are "tissues of fictionality.") So I wonder if it's preferable, or at least more critically fruitful, to think of him as a stochastic collage of moods and impulses, fragments of an unhinged unconscious patchworked together — into something that resembles a wandering interiority.

Either way, *Hunger* is a pre-Freudian swim in the depths of a troubled unconscious, a headfirst dive into uncharted psychological waters. It's a text before its time. In the preface to *The Cultural Life of Modern America* (1889), a biting critique of the New World that Hamsun published upon returning from his second and final trip to the United States, he argues that "truth telling is unselfish inwardness" — a position that calls to mind Søren Kierkegaard's oft-quoted epistemological inversion, anti-Enlightenment and for its time radical: "Truth is subjectivity" and "subjectivity is truth."

In *Hunger*, Hamsun tries to tell the truth by looking inward and only inward; the novel is a masterwork of navel-gazing. In the introduction to the 1967 translation of *Hunger*, Robert Bly envisions Hamsun as an "inward astronomer":

> An idea or an impulse rises above the horizon like a moon: Hamsun watches its whole course carefully, like an inward astronomer, convinced we have been too casual in watching the movements of the "heavenly bodies" or demonic bodies inside.

The narrator of *Hunger* is also an inward astronomer, hypersensitive of his own heavenly and demonic bodies, yet he, unlike the author who made him, can't control their cosmic course. He doesn't even try. The narrator observes his inward bodies come and leave, and he does not judge them, morally or otherwise. Often he acts upon them. In one scene, the narrator, "excited and drunk" and in such a good mood that his head feels full of "pure light," stops "abruptly" at a row of carriages for hire and climbs into one and shouts a made-up street name. Suspicious that the driver will infer from his "miserable clothes" that he's too poor to pay his fare, which he is, the narrator finagles a free ride out of the driver by convincing him that his trip is "a matter of life and death." Then he lies incessantly:

> I leaned back in the carriage, a prey to the maddest impulses, crept down under the oilskin hood so that no one would see me moving my mouth, and let myself go, chattering idiotically with myself. Insanity flooded through my brain again and I let it come, fully aware throughout of being under the influence of powers I could not control.

Similarly, in perhaps the most disturbing scene of all, the narrator, momentarily maddened by hunger, bites his own finger.

"The road of excess leads to the palace of wisdom," writes William Blake in *The Marriage of Heaven and Hell*. "You never know what is enough until you know what is more than enough." It would be naive, not to mention highfalutin (a word that sounded Norwegian to me until I learned the language), to say that by excessively obeying the heavenly and demonic bodies inside him — his moods and impulses and base desires — the narrator achieves wisdom, though he does achieve self-awareness, at least. And this he does at the expense of the other characters, all minor. His inner cosmos is, for him, the only cosmos. So truth-telling might be unselfish inwardness, but in *Hunger*, unselfish inwardness makes for selfish behavior. If anyone likes to play literary drinking games, here's a fast one: drink every time the narrator of *Hunger* hurts another character.

The narrator of *Hunger*, who is often deemed a "Nietzschean hero," might be beyond good and evil, or he might just be evil. Isaac Bashevis Singer notes in his own introduction to Bly's translation of *Hunger* that "Hamsun was perhaps the first to show how childish the so-called grownups are. His heroes are all children — as romantic as children, as irrational, and often as savage." *Hunger*'s hero is all of the above, with added emphasis on "savage" — or, a less problematic term, "cruel." *Hunger* prompts readers to ask: what would happen if a young and starving wannabe male writer obeyed his inward bodies, without consideration for other people?

So it's easy to see why another young wannabe writer, in need of a reason to feel special, incapable of distancing himself critically from what he reads, let alone separating art from life, would find *Hunger* so intoxicating. *Hunger* is a quintessential young writer's novel. It's like Joyce's *A Portrait of the Artist as a Young Man*, just less known and Scandinavian and therefore more mysterious. These days, TV viewers are fascinated by the figure of the Successful Sociopath — Tony Soprano, Walter White, the guy on *The Blacklist*. One theory is that this figure is the ego ideal of the neoliberal age: (s)he is selfish, unempathetic, socially strategic, and guilt-free — qualities suited for accumulating capital. The narrator of *Hunger* fascinated my adolescent self for an eerily similar reason: he is selfish, delusionally ambitious, self-absorbed, and guilt-free — qualities suited for making art. *Hunger* suggested to my adolescent self that I could be a little shit, so long as I did it for capital-A Art.

These are dangerous, not to mention stupid, thoughts for a young mind to be thinking. *Hunger*'s narrator, a wandering id, became for my naive adolescent self an ego ideal. *Hunger* changed me. I loved it so much that upon graduating I moved to Oslo, where I'd never even visited. It was either grad school or Oslo, and I guess I wanted to take the road less traveled by, or some other cliché like that.

Hermann Hesse called Hamsun his favorite writer. Charles Bukowski deemed Hamsun the greatest writer to have ever lived. Hemingway recommended Hamsun to Fitzgerald. Henry Miller called Hamsun "the Dickens of my generation." Thomas Mann described Hamsun "as a descendant of Fyodor Dostoyevsky and Friedrich Nietzsche." André Gide thought Hamsun was "perhaps even more subtle" than Dostoyevsky. Isaac Bashevis Singer claimed that "the whole modern school of fiction in the twentieth century stems from Hamsun, just as Russian literature in the nineteenth century 'came out of Gogol's greatcoat.'" And these are only a handful of the writers (all male, not coincidentally) who revered the eccentric Norwegian. Hamsun was for some time a kind of literary demigod, in Europe and abroad. And he would have stayed that way, probably, had he never become a Nazi.

Yeah. First, though, some backstory. Knut Hamsun, née Knud Pedersen, was born into poverty in 1859, in a place in the Gudbrandsdalen Valley called Lom. A few years later, his parents "sold" him to his uncle in Hamarøy, north of the Arctic Circle, to work on the latter's farm. His uncle starved and beat his nephew, who felt at times suicidal. Once he hacked his own leg with an ax. Hamsun mostly educated himself. He read voraciously. In his teens, he escaped his uncle's farm and traveled back to Lom, where he tried to become a writer. He wrote messy works without success. He traveled to America on two separate occasions, both times in search of work.

The autodidact and aggressively atheistic Hamsun decided that he disliked the four leading Norwegian writers of the time: Henrik Ibsen, Jonas Lie, Alexander Kielland, and Bjørnstjerne Bjørnson. Upon returning to Scandinavia from his final visit to the New World, Hamsun — evidently unafraid of conflict, and maybe also wanting to imbue his name with the electric heat of controversy — went so far as to give lectures where he personally lambasted the four of them one by one. Ibsen, then 63, heard about Hamsun's spite, was upset, and sat in the front row at Hamsun's lecture in Oslo (at the time called Kristiania). Yet Hamsun didn't fall shy. Hamsun said, with Ibsen glaring at him, that Norway's greatest playwright had a "coarse and spurious" psychological understanding of the stage. In Hamsun's mind, Ibsen's characters were "types," unrealistic and too coherent. Hamsun dreamed of a literature more inward and unpredictable. "I dream of a literature with characters in which their very lack of consistency is their basic characteristic," he wrote in a letter. "What interests me," he wrote elsewhere, "are my little soul's endless emotions, the special, strange life of the mind, the mysteries of the nerves in a hungry body." Hamsun realized these

SAYRE GOMEZ
UNTITLED PAINTING IN OFF WHITE W/TROMPE L'OEIL LAMP, 2015
ACRYLIC ON CANVAS
84 X 60"
COURTESY OF SAYRE GOMEZ AND GALERIE NAGEL DRAXLER
PHOTOGRAPHY: CHANEL VON HABSBURG-LOTHRINGEN

dreams and interests, of course, in *Hunger*, his first and arguably best novel. Although *Pan* (1894) — which Jeffrey Frank calls a "short, sexy, lyrical novel filled with hints of the supernatural," and which includes a hilariously odd scene where the unreliable first-person narrator, Lieutenant Glahn, is so overcome by "an absurd feeling of joy" that he falls on his knees and "in humility and hope" licks blades of grass — comes close.

These days, Hamsun is almost forgotten, at least in North America, and when he is remembered, he's remembered not for being an artist but a Nazi — a fully fledged, unrepentant Nazi. In Wood's apt words, "Some writers refuse to lay their heads peaceably on the pillow of literary history in order to give posterity good dreams." Hamsun supported what he called the "friendly" German invasion of Norway and endorsed Goebbels and Hitler, going so far as to welcome Hitler into his own house. After Hitler committed suicide, Hamsun wrote him a eulogy: "He was a warrior, a warrior for mankind, and a prophet of the gospel of justice for all nations." In Scandinavia, some bookkeepers still to this day refuse to sell Hamsun's works because they consider him a traitor. When I lived in Oslo — where, by the way, I made few friends, found no stable job, and spent nearly all my time claustrophobically alone, online, and depressed, or at least vitamin D deficient — I learned early on that even saying Hamsun's name was all but taboo.

So I wondered — I was forced to wonder — almost as soon as I arrived in Oslo: Wait, why am I here? Why was I moved, literally by literature (as in, I moved to Oslo because of Hamsun's book), by an author who in his old age became a Nazi? Does an author's senile conservative politics taint the radical works he composed in his youth? Why do I think of Oslo as a kind of muted, salt-water-taffy-colored dreamland, on the edge of some better, mysterious world, vaguely deathlike? Are my reasons for moving here artistic, or are they political? Oh, wait. Can I even separate the two?

In Oslo — a "strange city," as the narrator of *Hunger* observes, that "no one escapes from until it has left its mark on him" — I learned to look inward, like an "inward astronomer," but I did not look only at the "heavenly" or "demonic bodies inside." I learned to look also at my own inherited biases, my unchecked privileges, my ideological naiveties. In Oslo, I looked inward and, paradoxically, saw myself from a critical distance. I saw that my inner bodies were a faint part of a larger cosmos, historical and constructed. And from this critical distance, I saw myself as someone I should not treat seriously, someone to laugh at, not with, someone so ridiculous as to nearly be a cartoon.

And as it is in life, so too it is in reading. The less seriously I take myself, the better I become at reading, the better I become at treating texts as both serious and as seriously playful, seriously funny. There's a scene in Sheila Heti's *How Should a Person Be?* where the narrator and her best friend discuss "what you need to know in writing and what you need to know in art," and they come "to the same conclusion: you have to know where the funny is, and if you know where the funny is, you know everything." Heti, here, is clearly being hyperbolic; knowing where the funny is in x doesn't actually mean you know "everything" about x. Yet knowing where the funny is in x does add to a reader's understanding of x. And to know where the funny is in x, a reader must see it from a certain critical distance. "Comedy is tragedy plus time," sure, but comedy is also tragedy plus critical distance.

Hunger, I see now, is funny. Its narrator is so thunderously moody and impulsive and delusional that he, much like my adolescent self, is all but cartoonish. Here he is wandering Karl Johan, a main street in Oslo's downtown core (now a major shopping district), at night:

> I unconsciously checked my pockets for two kroner. The sexual energy visible in all the gestures of those going by, even in the dim flame of the gas lamps, and the motionless steamy night had all begun to affect me — this air filled with whispers, embraces, hesitant confessions, half-pronounced words, tiny squeals. Even the cats were making love with high-pitched shrieks in the door of Blomqvist's Café.

In Part IV, the narrator, so hungry he's "close to total collapse," slumps against a house wall by the corner of Tomte Street and watches a wholesale grocer's cart pass by:

> I saw it was filled with potatoes, but out of fury, from sheer obstinacy, I decided that they were not potatoes at all, they were cabbages, and I swore violent oaths that they were cabbages. I heard my own words very well, and I took the oath again and again on this lie, and swore deliberately just to have the delightful satisfaction of committing such clear perjury. I became drunk over this superb sin, I lifted three fingers in the air and swore with trembling lips in the name of the Father, the Son, and the Holy Ghost that they were cabbages.

Hamsun described "the hero" of his novel *Mysteries* as "a poseur, a pathological phenomenon, who is part madman and part genius." The narrator of *Hunger* matches this description, though he's also "inadvertently funny." I can never tell if he's messing with me. I can never tell if he's laughing at or with me, or at or with himself. Sometimes reading the book feels like reading one big inside joke I'm not a part of, and I can imagine Hamsun maniacally chuckling to himself as he wrote it. At his most tragic, the narrator is also most comical, and at his most comical, the narrator is also most tragic. He's both at once.

Hunger shares much in common with *The Comedy* (2012), a polarizing and perhaps needlessly offensive film by Rick Alverson about an unhinged young man, Swanson (Tim Heidecker, here solemn), who wanders through a city, Brooklyn, looking inward at his own heavenly and demonic bodies, and selfishly obeying them without consideration for others. *The Comedy* can even be treated as an inventive filmic adaptation of *Hunger* in contemporary Williamsburg.

Three obvious and arguably superficial differences between *Hunger* and *The Comedy*: *Hunger* is set in 1890s Oslo, *The Comedy* in contemporary Williamsburg; *Hunger* is about a poor and starving homeless Norwegian writer who lacks ties to family, *The Comedy* about a super-privileged American hipster about to inherit his dying father's estate; and the narrator of *Hunger* wants to become a writer, whereas Swanson does not want to become anything. These differences aside, though, the two texts are uncannily similar. Here's a passage from Wood's essay on Hamsun in the *LRB* that applies equally to *The Comedy*:

> In Hamsun, characters provoke apparently pointless encounters which they then disown or annul at whim. They are epistemological brawlers, always challenging meaning to a fight. They invent the scenes through which they move, and thus invent themselves afresh on every page. [...] [T]hey carry no continuous memory of what they have said or done from scene to scene. They seem only to be escaping themselves.

Swanson invents conflict in nearly every scene, and he never seems to remember what he's done, or feel guilty. At the beginning of the film, we learn that Swanson's comatose father is dying, but Swanson doesn't seem to care. Beside his father's deathbed he eats cookies, drinks scotch, and jokes around to the bug-eyed, nonresponsive male nurse about a prolapsed anus. Then he asks,

> So you change my dad? You put diapers on him and clean his asshole and put his shit in a bag, throw it out, put it down the toilet? Pretty cool, pretty cool way to live. I wonder if my dad's shit has ever gotten under your fingernails, and then you forgot, and you're driving home, worrying about your life, and you start biting your fingernails, and shit gets in your mouth?

Afterward Swanson leaves his father's mansion, skipping and singing like a cynical Shirley Temple down a posh flight of stairs, and joins a group of gardeners, all people of color, outside another affluent house nearby. He removes his shirt, kneels upon the soil, and slums it with the gardeners. When the (white male) owner of the house approaches, accompanied by the (white woman) landscape architect, Swanson asks, "It's coming along, huh?" The landowner and architect try politely to ignore Swanson, but he continues. He says that "his guys" who "don't speak any English" keep asking in Spanish if they can swim in the pool. "Why not?" replies the owner, perhaps so that Swanson will leave him alone. And Swanson, disappointed by the lack of conflict, abruptly walks away.

In one scene reminiscent of the one in *Hunger* where the narrator impulsively climbs into a taxi and orders the driver to take him to a nonexistent address, a drunk and sleepy Swanson hails a cab and offers the driver $400 to drive it around. At first the driver, Raj, ignores Swanson. Only after much cringeworthy arguing does Raj defend himself:

> Raj: Sir, this is not a playground. This is how I make a living.
> Swanson: I'm serious!
> Raj: This is my life.

> Swanson: I respect —
> Raj: I cannot let you —
> Swanson: Raj, Raj, this is just two gents, having a ride, talking about money, talking about business opportunities. Do you want to make $400 right now, and let me drive your cab?

Soon Raj agrees hesitantly to let Swanson drive for 20 minutes. Swanson drives cautiously at first, then speeds, slows down, and catcalls a woman walking alone. He asks, "How much?" Raj yells at Swanson, "Okay! Enough! Please, stop the car!" Swanson flips for the first time in the film: "SHUT THE FUCK UP!" he yells at Raj. The woman on the street approaches Swanson. "You think I'm a fucking prostitute?" she asks, and Swanson, momentarily exhilarated, ditches the car and sprints away, beaming.

Swanson could easily lounge about all day, doing nothing, but that would be boring, so instead he seeks out imaginative ways to be cruel. (I should mention that about halfway through the film, Swanson picks up a part-time job as a dishwasher, which might suggest some hope that he'll change.) He doesn't believe in the importance of other people. He doesn't really believe in anything. He's something of a nihilist. "Those who are most removed from concerns with how to survive find nihilist philosophies the most appealing," writes Whitney Mallett in a recent piece on D-accelerationism. Swanson, who lives off a trust fund and sleeps on a boat in Upper Bay, doesn't believe in anything because he can choose not to believe in anything and get away with it. The law, after all, serves to protect the powerful and privileged, and Swanson ticks off both boxes.

Swanson is no artist, but he is a kind of anti-artist, insofar as he creatively destroys other people. (It seems to me that when some creative people are miserable and can't create, they instead destroy, broadly speaking. So another way to view Swanson is as an artist without an art.) Yet even when he messes with someone he considers an equal, there's something hollow to it, something despondent. Watching *The Comedy*, I feel a croaking emptiness in my stomach. Does Swanson feel this way also? Heidecker's prodigious performance suggests that he does. His face on the poster for the film is his face throughout. Drunk eyes, a spoiled frown, a kind of perpetually repressed sob: this is the face of rich white American male *Weltschmerz*. Swanson's a miserable, perhaps suffering, person. Also, he's an evil person. Not beyond good and evil, like the narrator of *Hunger*; Swanson is simply evil. In the most disturbing scene of all, Swanson invites a much younger woman — a colleague at the café where he dish-washes — to his boat, offers her drinks and weed, jokes around, then watches as she has seizures. He doesn't offer help. He doesn't say anything. He merely sits and watches, looking bored.

The road of excess — which is, of course, typically reserved for the privileged, because the privileged can afford it — might lead to the palace of wisdom, yet for Swanson, unlike the narrator of *Hunger*, the road turns out to be a dead-end. Both *Hunger* and *The Comedy* end at the sea. In *Hunger*, the narrator boards a boat in the harbor and leaves Oslo. In *The Comedy*, Swanson merely splashes about with a grinning boy on the beach. Hamsun's heroes are all children, and Alverson's antihero is also a child — a man-child. The final scene of *The Comedy* is the only scene where Swanson looks happy, regressing into what he is.

Hunger prompts readers to ask: what would happen if a young and starving wannabe male writer living in late-19th-century Oslo obeyed his inward bodies, without consideration for other people? *The Comedy* prompts viewers to ask: what would happen if a young and privileged hipster living in contemporary Williamsburg obeyed his inward bodies, without consideration for other people? But there's another crucial difference: *The Comedy* isn't funny. Swanson and his like-minded friends — played by Eric Wareheim, James Murphy, Gregg Turkington, and Jeffrey Jensen — are too unsympathetic to laugh with (at least without feeling implicated in their cruelty). They occasionally make okay jokes, but they make these jokes at the expense of less privileged others. In one long scene, Swanson and three friends sit in an opulent Roman Catholic church, illuminated by candles, and sing fake Latin ("dominatrix") while other people — once again many people of color — pray. (I wouldn't be surprised if Alverson's go-to directions went something like, "Be as much of an oppressive asshole as you can, Tim.") The way Swanson and his friends live and act, it's all real and relevant — offensively so, even. But the disturbing reality is that if Swanson were a person — and it's both easy and tempting to imagine him as one — he wouldn't be that extraordinary. He'd be much like numerous other self-absorbed oppressive entitled men who abuse, might abuse, or will continue to abuse anyone unlike them, without consequence. (One criticism of the film is that we don't need to be reminded that such men exist.) So I wonder, is it even possible, in this case and in others, to separate the character from the person, or is it actually *more* critically fruitful to treat the character as both at once, somehow?

Identifying with a fictional character and treating him as a role model is naive, of course. Art is not life, and characters are not people. Yet the two do overlap. So, I've come full circle. My big questions now are pretty much the same ones I was asking at 19, stoned and flipping through the hierophanic *Hunger* and uncritically identifying with its unhinged narrator. How do I unyoke art from life, and should I? How do characters and people, art and life, eclipse each other? And how do I observe this eclipse, with what tools and from what vantage? The cosmos is expanding, in art and in life also, and inward bodies are beginning to look awfully slight, in the vast scheme of things.

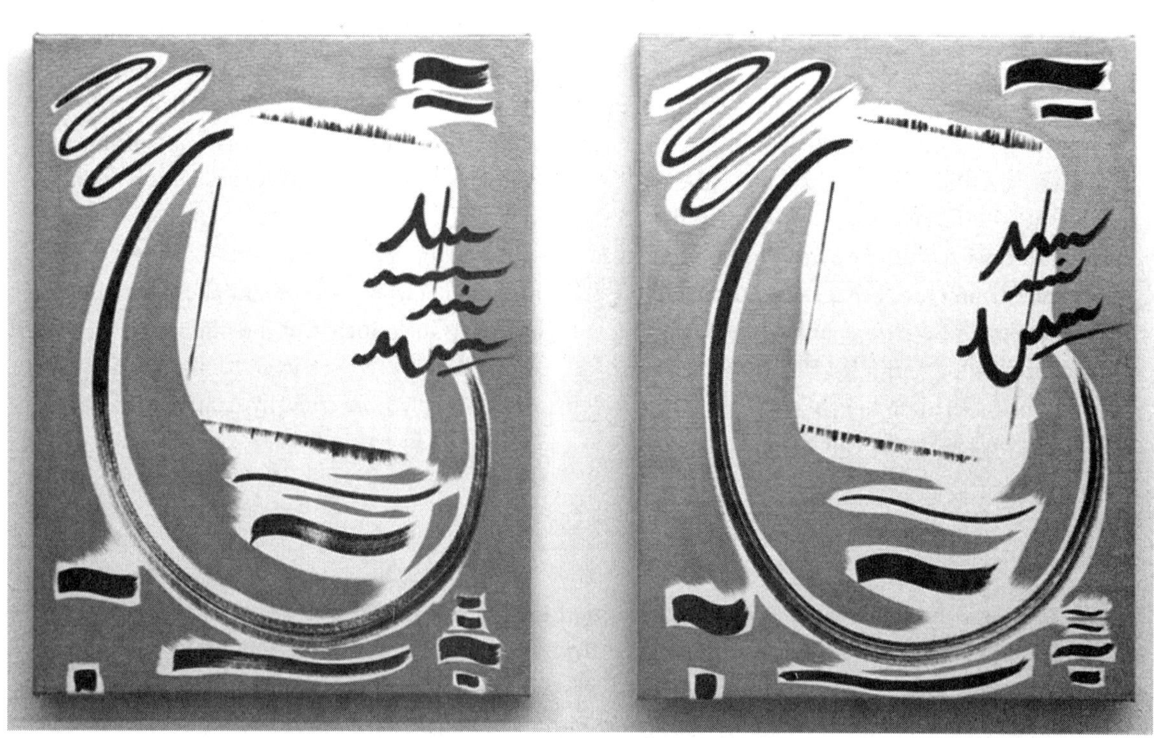

ALEX OLSON
JANE BIRKIN AUTOGRAPH (1/2, 2/2), 2009
OIL ON LINEN

Corruption GREG GLAZNER

THE GUEST LECTURER talks methodically and cheerfully, as willfully serene as the voice track of a mortuary commercial, looking toward the small auditorium's back wall, pacing the carpet, his hands clasped together in front of him, a short, stocky man of about 50 dressed in a black suit and what looks to be a priest's collar. The youngish, puffy look of his face and his willfully soothing way of speaking are at alarming odds with the grip his short hands keep on themselves. A brief biographical note provided by the Religious Studies Department describes him as an "unaffiliated scholar of theology with advanced degrees in Skinnerian Hermeneutics." Father Livermore, he calls himself, though there's no listing of a priesthood anywhere in his bio.

"Your feelings shift around every 15 seconds or so. No need to worry much with them," he says. He pauses a while. Students look up from their pages.

Livermore has stopped pacing and is smiling into the rows of freshmen. "Reason, though, can see a thing clearly, without the fuzz all over it." He looks down to make sure of his position, starts pacing again. "See, reason sights things cleanly and directly. It's as straight as the layout of a shotgun shack," he says cheerfully. "Anybody know what a shotgun shack is?"

There's a tense, general silence. *PhD*, the bio sheet says, then *Licensed Clergy (inactive)*.

"Well, if you go back into the Kentucky woods, the moonshiners can explain to you it's a narrow shack that's so straight, you can shoot a shotgun in through the front door and out through the back without hitting anything."

Students stare at him or slump back down to their notes.

"Yeah," he says cheerfully, nodding, as if he's heard laughter. His willfully upbeat tone lasts through a quarter-hour of lecture on the general post-Christian downward spiral of things. There does not appear to be a great deal of breathing going on in the room.

He says, "Only a spiritual understanding can steady us. Emotion, sex, substances, these won't do. But you don't have to take it from me. It's not only the theological who understand this." He stops pacing again, his eyebrows raised but his mouth expressionless.

"I can't GET no satisFACtion," he says, nodding with each accented syllable, his hands clasped in front of him. "But I've TRIED. And I've TRIED. And I've TRIED. And I've TRIED. I can't GET no," he says serenely, smiling, nodding his head, "satisFACtion."

After Fernando Traverso

JEAN VALENTINE

NI UNO, NI OTRO
NOSOTROS
the rubbed heart
the black bicycle
stenciled on the wall

13/8/93
LORE TE AMO
- the awkward-leaning phone poles,
old men and women resting back
against the sky in blue chairs,

- some sort of opening, like the dream
last night, with you still living -
did you make the dream-opening? or who?
I will carry you. Your happiness.
I am coming.

To who I don't know.   Te amo.
This happiness. Old life,
I'm glad, all my rubbed life
I was found,
I was written on a wall, in air.

En honor a Fernando Traverso

JEAN VALENTINE

NEITHER ONE, NOR THE OTHER
US
el corazón calcado
la bicicleta negra
estarcida en la pared

13/8/93
LORE I LOVE YOU
- los postes telefónicos inclinados torpemente,
mujeres y hombres viejos reclinados
contra el cielo en sillas azules,

- una especie de apertura, como el sueño
anoche, contigo aún vivo
¿creaste esa apertura en el sueño? ¿sino quién?
Te llevaré conmigo. Tu felicidad.
Ya voy.

A quién, no sé.   I love you.
Esta felicidad. Antigua vida,
me alegro, toda mi vida calcada
me encontraron,
escrita en una pared, en el aire.

Translated by Curtis Bauer

OCCIDENTAL FANTASIA, IN WHICH THE AUTHOR TRAVELS TO CHINA TO REGARD COPIES OF WESTERN CITIES

STEVEN BELLETTO

I USED TO HAVE a theory that the purest expressions of national culture are found in places geographically removed from the originating country. I developed this theory by drinking and then being blearily impressed by the house talent in expatriate haunts around the world, where refugees from their native lands stake claims to be the representative men and women of their home tradition. In early 2014 in Lisbon, I spent the night digging not fado but Bill Corcoran and The Melting Pot, the foot-stomping Irish folk group at O'Gilins Pub out near the Cais do Sodré. Back in 2010, in Baga, Goa, after bending under vines and pushing back elephant ears, I stepped into crumbling colonial times at Casa Portuguesa, a low-lit restaurant whose fado seemed to surpass anything in all of Iberia. In 2001, during my backpacking days in Bangkok, we bought long pants expressly as passports into the Mandarin Oriental's Bamboo Bar, where we had fraternal feelings for the American belting out Louis Armstrong standards as raspy and double-edged as if Satchmo himself had been reincarnated on the gold-tipped banks of the Chao Phraya. In each of these cases — hearing the Irish in Portugal, the Portuguese in India, and the American in Thailand — it seemed to me that by virtue of their cultural isolation, exactly because there were not dozens of Guinness taps or fado cellars or chromed microphones to be crooned into, these performances carried an attitude of longing that made them better, stripping them of campiness and compromise. Never mind the long-standing political and economic entanglements that had led to these fortresses of privilege in the first place, I thought: take the local tipple seriously enough and such performances will seem to be suffused with a preternatural clarity of purpose.

As any half-thought theory will do, this one struck back. It happened in late June 2014 as I stood in a winding Austrian alley, slouching for a picture with a teenager. We posed, for what seemed too long a time, before a window display of fruits and other dry goods — Hahne Hula Hoops (the Teutonic Froot Loops), Poppies (Rice Krispies), Happy Day condensed milk, and packages of Runder Zwieback. There were other stores around, too: a violin shop, a children's clothier, an ice

PHOTOS BY STEVEN BELLETTO

cream parlor — but that particular storefront apparently seemed to the teenager the most atmospheric tableau in a place whose watchword was charm: nearby windows had fretworked boxes from which spilled wildflowers and sprays of edelweiss, and there was even an expansive public chessboard with pieces the size of five-year-olds. It was like Austria embodied, the quintessence of Austria, the Austria you would think of if you ever thought about *The Sound of Music*: wall colors tended toward light buttercream, lacquered shutters abounded, hand-worked signs were supported by lacey wrought-iron brackets. There were little bells hung daintily near doorways in case you wanted to call down a braided blonde for beer and pretzels. It was the platonic ideal of small-town Austria, oozing equal parts Alpine rustication and Hapsburger refinement.

The teenager smiled, patted me on the arm again, and commanded her friend to tap out more photos with her phone. I did my best to smile but kept sweating unphotogenically due both to the humidity, which seemed otherworldly, and the crowdlets that were beginning to clot the alley around us. Lots of tourists, strangers to us both, stopped to take our picture as we posed for her friend. Many had what looked like professional equipment, and were setting up tripods and adjusting safari-grade lenses as I flushed more deeply. As they angled to frame me with the trellis on the nearby building, it dawned on me that I was being viewed as local color, as a moment of serendipity to be captured because it would make their vacation photos distinctive. I stood out because I was the only non-Asian person in the vicinity. I'm including in this count all the tourists who wandered down side streets with their Gucci totes and shade umbrellas, all the shopkeepers and salespeople, none of whom spoke German, and all the couples, perhaps two dozen in all, who dressed in full wedding regalia to have their photos shot with the verdigris lake or compact cathedral as background. How did I wind up the only Caucasian in an Austrian village? Because the village was located not in the actual Alps, or even in Europe, but on the outskirts of Huizhou, China, two hours east of Guangzhou.

I had specifically sought out this place, the much remarked upon "copy" of Hallstatt, a real-life UNESCO World Heritage village overlooking its namesake lake in the Salzkammergut, roughly equidistant from Innsbruck and Vienna. The in-progress Chinese version had been getting attention in the European and American press as what *Der Spiegel* called a "Xeroxed Village." Other reports came in over the wire, always slightly incredulous, that a Chinese construction conglomerate was building Hallstatt "brick by brick" (as CNN said), faithful down to the most seemingly insignificant detail, somewhere in the hills beyond the lychee orchards in the very un-Alpine Huizhou. The mayor of Hallstatt was miffed but polite about it, and he clearly spoke for his constituents when he said he was worried that the town's cultural traditions were being plagiarized.

In 2013, I had read with fascination Bianca Bosker's *Original Copies*, about the trend of "architectural mimicry" in contemporary China, which is much more widespread than just the copy of Hallstatt. As she writes:

> The target of the replication program goes beyond architecture and construction techniques. In fact, the agenda is all-encompassing: to re-create not only the superficial appearance of Western historical cities, but also the "feel" — the atmospheric and experiential local color — of the originals through such devices as foreign names, signage, and lifestyle amenities.

Could it possibly be, I wondered, that these places really did reproduce the "feel" of the place being copied? If I went to Hallstatt 2 in Huizhou, would it be like going to Hallstatt 1 in Austria, which I passed through in 1997 on a scenic route from Paris to Cluj-Napoca? And if so, could it somehow be purer than the original, as uncompromised as those performances on which I'd hung my theory?

I sketched an itinerary, and set myself up with an interpreter, Aran. He was a 40ish, scholarly ombudsman who was absolutely fearless when it came to necessary evils like breaching security perimeters at our more exclusive destinations. ("If you stop there," he said after striding past a guard house, "they just start asking you all sorts of questions.") Aran joined me after my visit to Hallstatt 2, and we went to some of the more elaborate foreign-themed developments scattered throughout the vast suburbs of Shanghai and Hangzhou: Thames Town in the Songjiang District, Holland Village in Gaoqiao, Venice Water Town in Zhejiang province, and Tianducheng Development Center, a French-themed park-cum-housing complex replete with a 350-foot-tall Eiffel Tower, an approximation of the Apollo fountain at Versailles, and a whole "French Townlet" so obsessed with minutiae that it trucked in pigeons, confined to coops on quiet days, to be released when it is deemed necessary to make the mood especially aching and provincial. Granted, these places are far from the expat enclaves that had originally inspired my line of thought, but they did seem ripe for analysis. The developers tended to hire native architects and designers, and indeed the very thing that makes them distinctive is that they are supposed to distill foreignness to its essence, to exude a sense of Austrianness or Dutchness or Britishness.

That summer was an auspicious time to think about China's views of the world. Xi Jinping had been increasingly vocal about his vision of a New Silk Road stretching from Urumqi and Khorgas in Xinjiang province all the way through Iran, Iraq, Syria, Turkey, Bulgaria, Romania, the Czech Republic, Germany, and the Netherlands. The impetus was not exclusively economic development — although this was certainly the prime motivator — but also cross-cultural pollination: the state-run Xinhua News Agency started a regular feature detailing the "dreams" that would be realized with Xi's proposed trade belt, and English-language papers touted the "social fabric" that would bring Beijing together with places like Tashkent and Astana. Premier Li Keqiang had just returned from a trip to Greece, where he emphasized that both countries had glorious ancient pasts. Beijing was preparing for a visit by Angela Merkel — workers hung both Chinese and German flags from every CCTV-ed lamppost around the Forbidden City and Tiananmen Square. The most widely reported story in the beginning of July was that Japanese Prime Minister Shinzo Abe's cabinet had adopted a resolution allowing their military the right to "collective self-defense," a move the Party viewed as imperialist saber-rattling, and which coincided with an increase in op-ed pieces arguing that the Sea of Japan should be renamed the East Sea (also a pet point of many a Korean cartographer). As

I snapped photos of windmills, St. Mark's Square, and the Bristol Cathedral, I noted little interest in the States beyond certain brands and certain universities, but there were many events designed to court the less flashy corners of the world, such as the grand opening of the 5,000-Year Cultural Expo Park in Anhui province, which feted 13 foreign ambassadors, including those from Mauritius, Grenada, Malawi, Suriname, and Zambia.

China was obviously conscious of the US but pretended not to be, and was asserting itself globally with a studied nonchalance toward American power. Sure, Peng Liyuan would trade fashion tips with Michelle Obama, and Jack Ma would list Alibaba on the NYSE, but the real energy was directed toward other parts of the world, where China hoped to establish a cultural and economic dominance that would last a millennium. It is therefore inviting to say that the trend of building communities in the style of the European colonial powers at the height of their wealth and influence was an imperial move, a kind of reverse Orientalism — an Occidentalism — with which China could claim authority over the faded empires of the West. One could even justify such a claim through close comparison of, say, the real Apollo fountain at Versailles, whose horses are all half-submerged as they struggle from the water, and the copy at Tianducheng, whose horses prance almost completely out of the water, just their hind legs invisible, as if to proclaim it is China alone that could really launch the Sun King's celestial chariot.

There is probably much truth in this analysis, but it doesn't account for the feel of these places, what Bosker calls the "the atmospheric and experiential local color" toward which they strive. This is what I was interested in. As it turned out, perhaps unsurprisingly, the dominant feeling I experienced in these places was not a fuzzy sense of homecoming to the familiar but a combination of dislocation and absurdity — for although they all aimed for gravitas, their inevitable errors and inconsistencies would appeal to even the staunchest cynic's sense of the ridiculous.

Indeed, there was little texture of the originating cultures on evidence in these developments. Hallstatt 2 exhibits only a cartoon Europeanness: the wildflowers and edelweiss tend to be made of plastic, as are the fruits and vegetables on the grocer's shelves, and hardly any of the display windows fronted actual stores. People could buy ice cream or coffee at inflated prices, but there were no antiques or violins for sale, let alone basic dietary staples. The chessboard was really part of a water feature, and the pieces were immovable. But when you got close up and looked beyond the superficial likenesses, you could see what was really interesting, those particular assemblages of details that would clarify into what Joan Didion once called "irony accessible to even the most literal viewer."

Approaching Hallstatt 2, visitors encounter an imposing "Scenic Introduction," which proclaims in Chinese and English (but not German): "In this fairy land, you will find yourself in an Austria fairy tale. Welcome to Minmetals Hallstatt Town to enjoy the breathtaking view and feel the perfect integration of the authentic Austrian European exoticness, Chinese traditional culture and Lingnan culture." It was easy to dismiss such claims to perfected authenticity when many of the carefully planned vignettes were patently inauthentic: an iconic red phone box that symbolizes Britishness the world over, for instance, and a curated ceramics display featuring a cornucopia, gingerbread men, a headless rooster, and a French waiter holding a bottle of wine and two baguettes. Clearly these were not the best examples of "authentic Austrian European exoticness," and yet it seems wrong to dismiss them as inept in the same way it is wrong to harp on your local Chinese takeout place for purveying syrupy deep-fried schlock instead of the earthy and layered dishes found in dozens of regional Chinese cuisines. The observation is accurate but misses the point of Chinese takeout.

My favorite moment in Hallstatt 2 was seeing a hand-painted sign advertising daily specials for a nonexistent Meeresfrüchte Speiselokal — Seafood Diner onto which was tacked, sublimely, a Chinese takeout menu from Horizon City, Texas, and one from a pizza place in Miami. These are the moments that do not merely take you out of the illusion you are in Austria — there are a thousand reminders of such — but that are so wrong they border on the transcendental. This was irony accessible to even the most literal viewer, yes, but it was also the purest expression of that exact cultural space — Minmetals Corporation Hallstatt-in-Huizhou, not Hallstatt — a specificity that demanded that people not compare it to the original, that they abandon notions of "original" and "copy" altogether. There is a zaniness in such moments, but one that bears the marks of history, of colonial encounter and global capital, and most of all of circulation, the theme of the 21st century, broadcast by menus of ethnic foods adjusted for American palates serving as substitutions for local Austrian seafood specials impossible to order in a brand-new ancient Alpine village in China.

On the side of the road near Holland Village, an older development in Gaoqiao, about an hour's drive from the center of Shanghai, there was a huge wooden clog and plaque explaining in Chinese and English (but not Dutch) that Holland's "treasures" are "Wooden shoes, tulip, windmill and cheese," a fact confirmed not only by that gargantuan "wooden" shoe, actually made of resin, but also by the presence across the canal of a windmill straight out of any Delftware tile you could buy in tasteful Schiphol. Being older, Holland Village drew no tourists, and unlike Hallstatt 2, where I had been photographed like a celebrity, I encountered only two people on the streets as I stalked various points of interest for several hours. The lengthiest conversation I had was in the sales office — I visited the sales office in each development, from the glitziest, in Hallstatt 2, with its leather club chairs and hostesses dressed in dirndls, to Thames Town's bare rooms with folding chairs and mimeographed maps with purchased properties X-ed out. In Holland Village, where unbuilt phases were already being sold, the sales office was first-rate: we were greeted by bowing doorwomen, a daycare corner, and lighted acrylic models as impressive as those in Huizhou; a sloppily tied 22-year-old sales associate beamed a laser pointer over the location of future schools, malls, vegetable stalls, and major roadways. He tried to sell me on one of the four-story villas planned for phase II, the garden of Holland Village, for around 55,000 yuan ($8,860) per square meter. "It's romantic," he kept saying. "Romantic and convenient." I wasn't exactly sold on the romance part, even though the windows of the sales office likewise promised: "The world's most bustling and romantic streets, in Nederland."

I was sold, however, on those moments of particularity best illuminated by a robust sense of irony. The entrance to the Holland Village Hatha Yoga Center, for example, was plastered with two huge-bearded smoker dolls, one of whom held a sign reading ERZGEBIRGE — wholly appropriate as smoker dolls come from that region in Germany — and was emblazoned with JOYFUL and CHILDHOOD and FUNNY, a collision of cultural quotations so strange that it was hard to suss out the thought process that led to a blending of traditional Indian practice (in its trendy Santa Monica–approved version), creaky Old World kitsch, and a vaguely Christmassy, F.A.O. Schwarz / *Babes in Toyland* ethos reminiscent of a mythical middle-class American childhood. That none of this made sense in terms of Dutchness was beside the point. An elderly woman sweeping the sidewalk in front of a nearby preschool didn't know what hatha yoga was, and suggested I was wasting my time in Holland Village. I asked if she felt at all like she was in the Netherlands, pointing to the windmill and canals, the buildings with stepped gables, narrow facades, and little inset blocks, called *gevelstenen*, explaining that they were "opgericht in 2005." She shrugged and said merely that the buildings looked nice. Which was true enough.

Because Aran understood I was interested in architectural copies, he suggested a detour to Shanghai Film Park, the city's watered-down version of Universal Studios, where many a real Chinese film has been made. I wanted to go straight to Thames Town, but Aran argued that if I was interested in Chinese copies of Western buildings, then what could be better than a real working back lot, where set designers oversaw the construction of structures so realistic they are used in the movies? I started to explain why it seemed to me qualitatively different to experience a copied place that was built for people to live in versus a copied place that was built as a movie set. The latter seemed phonier to me. But Aran handed me a brochure that explained why 1930s Nanjing Road was the centerpiece of the Film Park: it "remains faithful to the old architecture and offers high human and historical value. It is highly regarded by academics in architecture and history in the City of Shanghai." He looked at me and spread his palms: QED. So we went to Shanghai Film Park, which cost me 80 yuan, but Aran got in free because he had a special government card.

It was fun, at first, to pretend I was walking around in the opening sequence of *Indiana Jones and the Temple of Doom*, but as the drizzly mist became a full-fledged rainstorm, my feeble travel umbrella no haven, it became evident that the imaginary city council or central committee had failed to plan for real-life downpours. The rickety cobbled streets and narrow sidewalks were soon overtaken by vast puddles and mini-lakes, and I got profoundly drenched. My shoes and socks were soaked through, and the hypochondriac in me starting visualizing trench foot and its attendant problems. We hunted down the largest-sized rubber sandals we could find (which were still too small) — the same model Aran and a great many others wore.

I had to hand it to Aran: the architecture was impressive, even as there was no pretense of the structures being anything more than facades. The few tourists braving the weather were enjoying the only "ride" at Shanghai Film Park, an old-timey tram that looped around faux Nanjing Road. "The tram car itself is a sight in motion," waxed the brochure. "It looks exactly like the originals. When you take a tour on the tram car, you will feel that you are passing through a time tunnel and returning to the dreamy old days." Who isn't a sucker for the dreamy old days? I rode the tram, which from the outside was a fairly accurate reproduction of the electric trolleys used in Shanghai since the 1910s: we poked along Nanjing Road, the rain blasting in sideways through the open windows, no commentary from the driver. The whole trip lasted about 10 minutes, and it took us on the route I had already seen on foot. A couple of days later, coincidentally, the city decommissioned its last remaining trolley buses, which had run in parts of Shanghai for 100 years. The forward-looking city marked the occasion with minimal fanfare, just a cadre of enthusiasts who coordinated a farewell ride on the No. 14 trolley bus.

When at last we arrived in Thames Town, the first thing we came across was the familiar-looking Tram Bar, a snack shack constructed to look like a repurposed vehicle of the same family as the dreamy old tram I had just ridden through the 1930s. From what I could tell, it was not actually a repurposed trolley bus but was built from scratch. It nevertheless lent Holiday Square the impression that an industrious entrepreneur had refurbished a defunct means of conveyance to sell candy floss and flavored ice, something one might find at a real English holiday spot like Brighton

Pier. Unfortunately, as in Holland Village, there was hardly a soul to be seen in Thames Town, and the Tram Bar was padlocked, its awning bulging dangerously with rainwater.

The deluge had mellowed to gray drizzle, which did much for the British mood, but also created an unsettling feeling — not quite eerie, but hushed and forsaken. This atmosphere was heightened by the lack of people and by the many statues that had been worked into the hardscape by the designers. These were generally not monuments on pediments — although there were exceptions, such as Florence Nightingale and someone who was either Charles Dickens or Charles Darwin — but were rather human-sized and situated around Thames Town as if they were real humans. I had seen this phenomenon before in Holland Village, where there was a lone human-sized statue on the curb near the sales office, a man in a business suit holding a briefcase and checking his watch, as if waiting for a train. Thames Town elevated this feature to a different plane: there were statues everywhere, dapper ladies and gents sitting on benches who were dressed as though they had just stepped out of Bloomsbury between the wars; there was a youth in the act of either declaiming or eating (impossible to tell what the lump in his hand represented); there was even a Lord Byron–looking fellow who lounged horizontally on the banks of the tractor-dug River Thames, with a great mane of hair and an open book. All this was unsettling because there were many more statues than people, and they were positioned as a kind of permanent Madame Tussauds in bronze. A mild-mannered graduate student, bow-tied and bespectacled, waited for you on a public bench to have an imaginary conversation about something very British, like the HMS *Dreadnought* or wogs.

The centerpiece of Thames Town was called Old Town Square, which did have enterable amenities: a pet store, pub, coffeehouse, and one-off shops like Lilliputian and Scarecrow Handmade Soap. In the heart of Old Town Square, all cobbled streets, puffing chimneys, and half-timbered mock Tudor and Edwardian homes accented by black and gold-leafed lampposts, looking prim and Victorian, there was a large place called the Thames Bar. It was built behind a substantial colonnade, which created the effect of an arcade. Inside was a mahogany bar with brass railings and beer on tap, and lots of low tables and chairs with views of the street. Maybe it was the foggy drizzle or that I had come directly from Shanghai Film Park, but despite the borderline creepiness of the statues, at that moment Thames Town seemed to me the most successful of all the Western-style developments, if only because it managed to evoke a feeling of being elsewhere. It was a perfected version not of England, though, but of a colonial space in a distant land trying to capture a bygone era of romance and adventure, like the parts of Kenya or India where inky traces of Britishness lingered — it was a copy of a copy of an idea. Yet, strangely, you could luxuriate there, drinking gin and tonics and maybe playing a little cricket on the dartboard. You could even do rabbit ears behind the grumpy-looking statue of Winston Churchill out front. The onetime subjects had outdone the empire.

—

Thames Town had put me in an anglophone frame of mind, and as I was winding down my travels through copied cities and preparing for Katie's arrival — she was flying in direct from Newark to join me for other kinds of sightseeing — I thought it would be a fitting capstone to book a room at the Fairmont Peace Hotel, the art deco gem on the Bund featured prominently in Shanghai Film Park's Nanjing Road. Katie arrived in the afternoon, and we walked the Bund, which is the truest expression of European architecture in all of China, had dinner, and stopped for a nightcap at the Jazz Bar in the Fairmont. Speaking of fortresses of privilege: the Jazz Bar was a storied hotspot going back to the 1920s, complete with a doorman to keep the lobby gawkers out. Inside, the place was dark, with massive stone columns and iron chandeliers that lent it the look of a medieval cloister — except for the long bar along one wall and the bandstand along the other. Part of the crowd was the same international set you would find at any upscale hotel bar in the world, but the majority were well-heeled domestic tourists, mainly couples who sat sullenly around their tables with intricate towers of untouched crudités and ice buckets of Veuve Clicquot.

We ordered wine and Sazeracs and looked forward to being blearily impressed by the house talent, the Old Jazz Band, famous because it was literally composed of old musicians, Chinese jazz veterans who ranged in age from late 70s to early 90s. They drew both domestic and foreign crowds, and had even had a documentary made about them the year before, which was advertised on the walls near the door. So it seemed appropriate to be sitting there at that moment, reunited with Katie and eager to hear masters of a music that was supposed to be one of the few art forms indigenous to the United States. The band was seated, holdovers from another age, with their white Humphrey Bogart dinner jackets and thinning hair combed and Brylcreemed. Chinese tourists got up from their tables and positioned themselves mere feet away, brandishing their smartphones expectantly. A table of Aussies continued their beery conversation. Of course I knew it was impossible to plagiarize a place, let alone a feeling or a mood, which are ineffable and fleeting anyway. And yet I also realized there was value in attending to those strange spaces that claimed to be what they are not, in relishing ironic disjuncture while admitting the authenticity of the places themselves. Katie and I ordered another round as the drummer raised his stick in the air, the trumpeter and saxophonist put mouthpieces to lips, took deep breaths, and began to play.

RADIO AND CHILD: WALTER BENJAMIN AS BROADCASTER

BRÍAN HANRAHAN

1.

A FEW YEARS AGO the BBC's flagship domestic station, BBC Radio 4 (imagine a better-funded NPR, with a more central place in national life), canceled its main children's show *Go4It*. Audience research had revealed — perhaps belatedly — that the average age of the listenership was well over 50. Maybe it was chastening for the program makers, maybe they knew it all along. Seen in longer historical perspective, however, the disjuncture is not so unusual. Of all mass media, radio has always had the least developed relation to children. The history of film or photography, of TV or the internet, could hardly be written without reference to the child: images of children, children as audience and market, children's actual or hysterically invoked vulnerability. But radio has always been an overwhelmingly adult phenomenon.

Of course, there has long been broadcast radio aimed at children. There were kids' serials in the American network golden age, cozy British stuff like *Listen with Mother* in the 1960s, various kinds of educational radio. There are Sirius satellite channels, and Radio TEDDY, a German children's broadcaster, still transmits on the airwaves. But all this — and even radio hardware marketed to children — is a small and relatively unimportant part of radio as a historical phenomenon. Moreover, radio's relation to children is indirect, even uncanny: for children, radio is above all something addressed to grown-ups, but they can overhear it, or listen in on it. Radio, in this way, becomes a channel to a world beyond the home. Voices and sounds from the radio bring traces of a different life into the cloistered spaces of childhood and family.

2.

Any serious history of children and radio — any history going beyond a chronicle of program offerings — must include the German writer Walter Benjamin. Benjamin wrote extensively for the radio, and most of those broadcast writings — now newly translated and collected — were written for children, at least at first glance. More than that, something quintessentially *Benjaminian* happens in that uncanny encounter of radio and child: the hint of an unsettling remainder in the everyday, in the dislocation of sent message and received meaning, in the figure of the child who knows something his parents do not.

Benjamin's texts date from the late 1920s and early 1930s, when he was a regular broadcaster on Berlin and Frankfurt radio, mostly for youth and children's programming. Benjamin's self-reinvention as a broadcaster was the product of necessity. Excluded from the academy, he made a living with prolific freelancing. He was well connected in literary circles, which overlapped considerably with the burgeoning German broadcast industry. Above all, radio work came his way through an old school friend, Ernst Schoen, head of the culture department of Frankfurt radio, the most liberal and aesthetically adventurous of Germany's nine regional stations.

As in much of Europe, early German radio was highly controlled and highly conservative. Although broadcast technology was a product of war's accelerated modernization, the new medium's ideology was rooted in paternalistic cultural politics. Planners of the first free-to-air stations foresaw a one-way transmission of high-to-middlebrow culture: edifying, mildly diverting programs meant to ease a quiescent population to sleep. The extraordinary energies of interwar popular culture — as seen in Weimar cinema or the illustrated press — were to be kept firmly outside, through a mixture of institutional culture and, if necessary, overt censorship. The restrictions extended to politics and current affairs: any mention of these, beyond the pieties of official nationalism, was tightly sequestered into a few short daily news bulletins, distributed by a central agency.

Paternalistic cultural statism — similar to the creed of John Reith, the BBC's founding father — quickly came into tension with commercial interests. Radio in Germany, as elsewhere in Europe and beyond, took off very rapidly in the 1920s. In just a few years, the early cottage industry developed into a highly capitalized commercial sector. There was much at stake in the sale of hardware and the provision of content — profits, reputations, and careers to be made. Huge modern broadcasting centers were built in major German cities. Receivers got steadily cheaper, technological innovation continued, and listener numbers quickly grew, as did daily broadcast hours. Without ever fully breaking out of the confines of the original model, Weimar radio became a looser, larger, and more modern phenomenon. Music — light and even popular music — took on a more important role, especially in the daytime, for a female audience. With the coming of synchronized film sound, movie hits were regularly played on air in a conscious attempt to maximize synergies between cinema and radio, including the sale of phonograph records and sheet music.

This was the labile world of late Weimar broadcasting in which Benjamin briefly found his niche. The bulk of his radio work comprised 20- to 30-minute talks written for an audience of young listeners. Along with travel pieces and a series on Berlin arcana, they include talks on a dizzying range of topics. Dipping into demotic history, Benjamin turns his attention to, among other things, swindlers and con men, robber bands and witch trials, gypsies and bootleggers, the Lisbon earthquake and the fall of the Bastille. The miscellany can be bizarre — a collection of anecdotes about dogs, for example, or a "brainteaser" broadcast with an incomprehensibly elaborate interactive quiz. There is also quite a bit of what, at first glance, reads like light feuilleton reportage, with Benjamin turning an acute journalistic eye — his instinct for detail serving him well — on factories, department stores, and street markets. These subjects rarely seem imposed from above. Instead, the broadcasts trace a whimsical wandering line in Benjamin's own thought. He seems to write about whatever is on his mind or on his reading table at the time.

In addition to programs for children, Benjamin turned out a few radio plays (some for kids, some not) as well as "grown-up" lectures on a variety of topics. At times, an astute freelancer, he lightly reworked already published content. His first ever radio talk was a report on "Young Russian Poets," using material from his time in Moscow; his last, just before the Nazi takeover, was a reading from his *Berlin Childhood Around 1900.* More significantly, he also wrote a number of didactic role-play vignettes on work and careers, so-called "listening models" heavily influenced by the epic theatre and the early media theory of Bertolt Brecht, with whom Benjamin enjoyed a close, if sometimes one-sided, friendship. In this mode, Benjamin sought to inject some political urgency, some sense of the present — some *actuality*, in the buzzword of the day — into the torpid banality of Weimar radio. The dialectical dialogue "A Pay Raise? Whatever Gave You That Idea!," for example, dramatizes correct and incorrect ways of asking for a pay raise.

In terms of his own finances, Benjamin did pretty well from all this work. Radio honoraria were probably his main income at the time. In fact, for a brief moment, Benjamin was a prototype of a later phenomenon, when public broadcasters effectively subsidized European literary production with generous broadcast fees. (Near the BBC's old HQ in London, you can still find pubs with pictures of George Orwell and Dylan Thomas displayed above the bar, celebrating the radio checks cashed and spent there.) But the wider question of the value of Benjamin's radio writings, and their place in his work, has never really been settled. For the most part, they have remained a vaguely known but ultimately obscure corner of his sprawling oeuvre.

The neglect was partly due to editorial taxonomy. Right or wrong, *medium* was not an organizational principle for Benjamin's early editors, so the broadcast writings were lumped in with other occasional and journalistic work. The absence of sound recordings also played a role. Early radio was overwhelmingly live, and went almost completely unrecorded. The problem was solved by around 1930 — 16-inch disk recorders became standard in-house technology. But the process was awkward and expensive, and only a fraction of programming survives. (Among other things, this means that there is no recording of Benjamin's voice, a lack that surely contributes to the aura of ineffability that clings to his persona.)

But the biggest stumbling block for later readers of the radio work is the vehemence with which Benjamin himself wrote it off. At the time, he privately dismissed his broadcast writing, with a few exceptions, as pure hackwork — *Brotarbeit*, "bread-work," he calls it — which sapped his energies, distracting him from more important tasks. In one letter to his friend Gershom Scholem, he reports that he has hired a new dictation secretary, to save time with the radio stuff, and literally to keep his hands clean. Critics writing about the radio work have done some neat footwork to get around this authorial dis-imprimatur. A 1990s monograph ingeniously suggested that the oral composition, and the strong association with childhood, meant the pieces could be read psychoanalytically, as emanations from Benjamin's unconscious. Others, correlating what he wrote about radio with his harsh judgment of his own radio writing, read him as a thwarted avant-gardist, forced to forego his experimental desires and modernist plans, reduced by circumstances to writing embarrassing lectures for children.

3.

Given this attitude, one might wonder at Verso's publication of a nearly complete and newly translated volume of the radio writing. It is tempting to hear the rattle of the spoon scraping the last from the

Benjaminian barrel. Being cynical about Benjamin is easy these days, after he has been overexposed by a joyless kind of academic hype, his reputation dulled by mechanical praise. But you only need to read him to be charmed and awed again. In fact, these little broadcast miniatures contain some of Benjamin's most delightful moments. The scale of his erudition is almost comical: the scholar of Kant and the connoisseur of the Baroque deploys his profound knowledge of the history of stamp collecting. Shaped for a young audience, more than ever his learning is worn with lightness and grace. And as always, his ideas are inseparable from images. In his talk on puppetry, Benjamin recalls performances witnessed in half a dozen cities, tells tales of puppets blowing smoke rings or turning into live doves, recounts shows called "The Robber Baron Flayed Alive!" and "Murder in the Wine Cellar." He quotes, fondly and verbatim, the patter of puppeteers, living and dead. But the images, no matter how full of wonder, are knitted together (*kneaded* together ...) in resolutely materialist and historical analysis, as he invokes puppetry's link to the sacred — through fetish and animism — and traces its history to the blasted aftermath of the Thirty Years' War.

It is as if Benjamin can't help himself. No matter what the audience, no matter how abstruse or mundane the subject, he cannot help — with a turn of phrase or a turn of thought — but reveal his dialectical finesse, his subtlety with images, his depth of imaginative recall, his aphoristic brilliance. Like a prince in disguise, he gives himself away. His little talk on Cagliostro — the 18th-century religious charlatan who conned his way around the courts of Europe — contains a subtle psychological reading of the man, and a critique, in passing, of narrow-minded Enlightenment. Deeply sympathetic to Cagliostro himself, Benjamin is scornful of the courtly dupes, so proud of their "Reason," who could neither see through nor ever understand his con:

> people were so firmly convinced the supernatural world did not exist, they never took the trouble to reflect upon it seriously and thus fell victim to Cagliostro. [...] This is another lesson from the story: in many cases, powers of observation and knowledge of human nature are even more valuable than a firm and correct point of view.

Benjamin turns and returns to the 19th century above all. As in *Berlin Childhood Around 1900*, images from his own childhood blend with a wider history. He alludes repeatedly to his teachers, his favorite books, his young adventures in the city. But the personal is not private. His childhood consciousness is invoked so its experience can resonate with other alert young minds, both in the 19th century and among his radio listeners. This complex communion is at its most crafted in talks devoted to toys. The "Berlin Toy Tour" essays are, on one level, a kind of feature journalism: Benjamin visits a department store, describing in detail the wonder of modern toys, and recalling those of his own youth. But the talks go strangely and beautifully astray, passing through a brief history of artisanal craftsmanship, then morphing into a reflection — a self-reflection — on the relation of passion, knowledge, and possession. He concludes in the simplest of voices:

> [...] it's left to me to calmly say what I really think: the more someone understands something, and the more he knows of a particularly kind of beauty — whether it's flowers, books, clothing or toys — the more he can rejoice in everything that he knows and sees, and the less he's fixated on possessing it, buying it himself, or receiving it as a gift. Those of you who listened to the end [...] must now explain this to your parents.

The image of children teaching their parents gives a hint of the radio essays' wider purpose. All in all, read together — as the Verso volume allows — his children's essays emerge as a coherent experimental project in its own right, but not in any strict sense a formal or technical experiment. Its modernism has little resemblance to the ideas of the early radio avant-garde, be it F. T. Marinetti's Italian noise poetry — influential then, still reverently cited today — or the Russian Futurists' invocation of a radio-planetary sublime. It is a world away from Brecht's best-known radio work, the modernist cantata *The Flight of the Lindberghs*, with its dramaturgy of closed-circuit transmission.

Instead, Benjamin's essays for children are an exercise in popular historical pedagogy, a serious attempt — at least to begin with — to give voice to a revitalized Enlightenment, colored with Benjamin's own idiosyncratic historical materialism. Benjamin, in other words, takes an unashamedly pedagogical approach, but one quite unlike the state paternalism that funneled a diluted high culture to a mass audience, in hopes they would quiet down and learn their place. His project here is to use radio's new public sphere to propagate an Enlightenment "from below," drawing energy from the force of a pre- and extra-capitalist popular culture.

This makes Benjamin's radio writing sound more abstract and highfalutin than it is. It was meant, after all, for children and adolescents. There is a startling lack of snobbery to the man, in content, tone, and technique. (How *game* he is. Imagine Adorno or Heidegger writing a quiz, or telling little stories about dogs.) His style is crafted with the radio medium in mind, not in some reified sense of "the acoustic" but as a device that enables him to address actual people, whom he presumes to be intelligent, already possessed of knowledge, and keen to gain more. Technique aligns with subject matter. Over weeks and months, never using his own name — but using "I" a lot — he builds a palpable radio persona, addressing his audience with informality and care. He even has a kind of catchphrase, beginning many of the talks with "Are you familiar with […]?" or "I imagine you must already be familiar with […]." At the end of broadcasts, he often offers gentle summaries, little teacherly pointers for further thought, or the suggestion — the hope, really — that the listener, in some future moment, may recall the talk and its writer.

The quiet performative élan guides the listener on a digressive but not aimless passage through the history of European popular culture. These talks amount to a portrait — a composite, occasional, and partial portrait — of *the people*. Images of children in the city blend with Benjamin's own longing — he was not alone in this at the time — for a literate, confident proletariat as a cultural and political force. Quoting Adolf Glassbrenner, chronicler of early 19th-century Berlin, he might be speaking of his own radio enterprise: "We are separated from the great mass of the people by everything, by eccentric habits and education, by money, by our speech, and by our clothes. Unless we join hands with the people and come to an understanding with them, no freedom is possible."

Benjamin's pickings from his trove of arcana — whether on puppets or Pompeii — are not representative moral fables, but are chosen for the life that flows through them, for populist cheerfulness, resourcefulness, and wit, for a glint of humor or pathos, for shrewdness leavened with generosity, for a nonpossessive worldliness. They are the embodiment, in tales recounted and lives lived, of a popular countertradition of wisdom, courage, and stubborn autonomy. All of this, it is clear, Benjamin felt it important to impart to the young. Put another way, these radio talks perform an unassuming version of the dialectical move Benjamin so loved: invoking a past first made strange and then made available, which feeds the present's imagination and fuels its courage.

4.

Why then Benjamin's negative judgment on what was, at least in part, clearly a labor of love? Why did he dismiss these popular pedagogical pieces and deny the effort he put into them? Shame explains it, in part: Benjamin's discomfort at his increasingly diminished social status led to a certain contempt — both banal and perverse — for commissioned work and residual professional affiliations. But it is also important to understand the ultimate trajectory of his radio career, which becomes clear in a collected volume. Reading the full series of radio talks, you get a sense of great energies gradually sapping away. The care and finesse of the early talks goes missing; the final broadcasts are hurried and slapdash, segues are awkward or broken, the choice of subjects increasingly arbitrary and unformed.

Clearly — and ironically, given his attention to high spirits and the transmission of resolve — Benjamin lost heart and lost interest. Maybe the work took an emotional toll he was no longer willing to pay. To bring pedagogical tenderness to bear is not easy at the best of times. Without recordings to play back, without a clear place — or a job — at the station, without any coherent channel for feedback, Benjamin must sometimes have felt as if he were speaking into a void. The short text "On the Minute" (strangely omitted in this book), an evocative account of panic and loneliness before the studio microphone, alludes to this sense of isolation.

But more direct political factors also played a role. A first jolt of authoritarianism centralized German radio in 1932, dragging it toward the nationalist right. Reactionaries scoured the stations, enforcing a stricter alignment with the state. And things got worse: Benjamin's last broadcast came in early 1933, a day before Hitler was appointed Chancellor. After that, there was no more radio for him. Goebbels — a different kind of radio artist — took over.

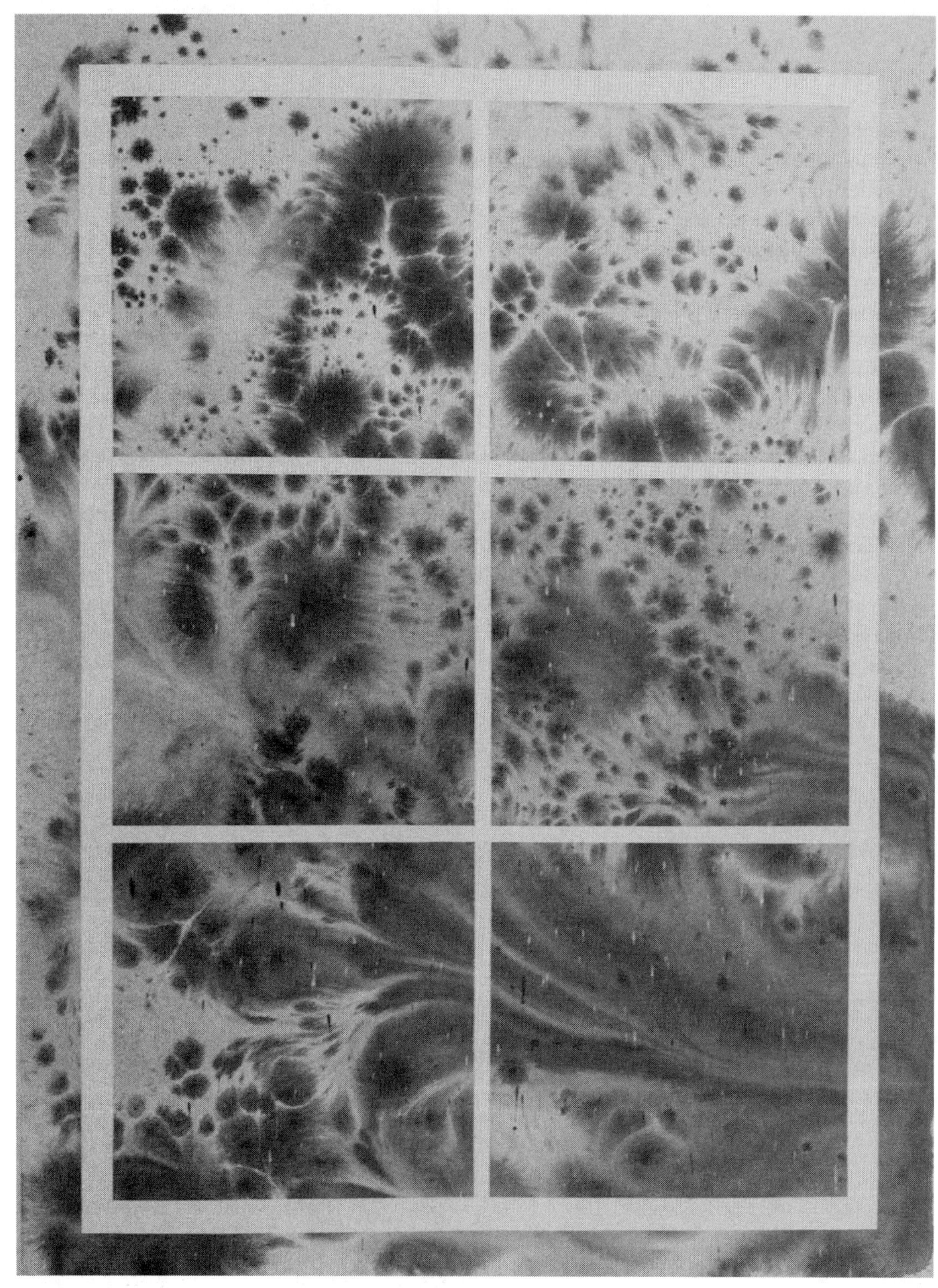

SAYRE GOMEZ
UNTITLED PAINTING IN WHITE WITH WINDOW MOTIF, 2014
ACRYLIC ON CANVAS
40 X 30"
COURTESY OF SAYRE GOMEZ AND GALERIE PARISA KIND

Death ROLF POTTS

THE STORY ON the bottom of the stack is called "Excavation," and it seems promising. Like the other stories, this one is focused on a death, but, unlike the others, "Excavation" appears to convey nuance. In it, a team of scientists is commissioned by the US government to bring home the remains of American soldiers from Vietnam. The team leader, Dean, conducts a dig on an old battlefield near Khe Sanh when he finds the remains of what appears to be an American body. The skeleton wears a high school class ring, and Dean begins to obsess about who the man was when he was still alive.

I wrote "Excavation" when I was 14 or 15 years old, and I rediscovered it almost three decades later in a box of old papers alongside other short stories I'd penned in the mid-1980s. Rendered in a studied imitation of Stephen King's prose, most of the stories are essentially a clever preamble to some sort of violent death. "The Highwayman," for instance, is about a chatty young couple that gets murdered when they stop their car to assist a creepy man at the side of the road. A revised version features the same chatty couple in the same car, only this time they kill the creepy man at the side of the road.

Two of the stories describe what appears to be a normal situation, only to reveal that death has already occurred. "Neighborhood" is about a skittish man who is trying to borrow eggs from his neighbors, none of whom answer the door when he knocks; by the end of the story we learn that his neighborhood has been ravaged by nuclear war. "Therapy" is about an arrogant psychiatrist who rants at an unresponsive patient; by the end of that story we learn that the therapist is insane, and the patient isn't responding because he's been stabbed to death with a letter opener.

In the longest story, "Funland," a young stoner sneaks into an abandoned amusement park to smoke LSD-laced weed. This throws the issue of death into question: is the evil clown really killing the boy by smashing his head into the calliope, or is the drug-addled teen doing it to himself?

By comparison, the protagonist's meditation on mortality in the early pages of "Excavation" feels almost Shakespearean. In the tale, Dean walks through the darkness of a stormy Southeast Asian night, wearing the dead man's class ring and trying to empathize with who the man might have been. This goes on for several paragraphs, in curiously specific detail, until we get the sense that the story's young author wasn't sure what should happen next.

Finally, around the middle of the fifth page, there's a breakthrough: the storm crescendos and Dean is struck by a bolt of lightning, sending him back through time to 1968, where he is killed by North Vietnamese Army soldiers.

In this way I am reminded, all these years later, that the body Dean had exhumed was in fact his own.

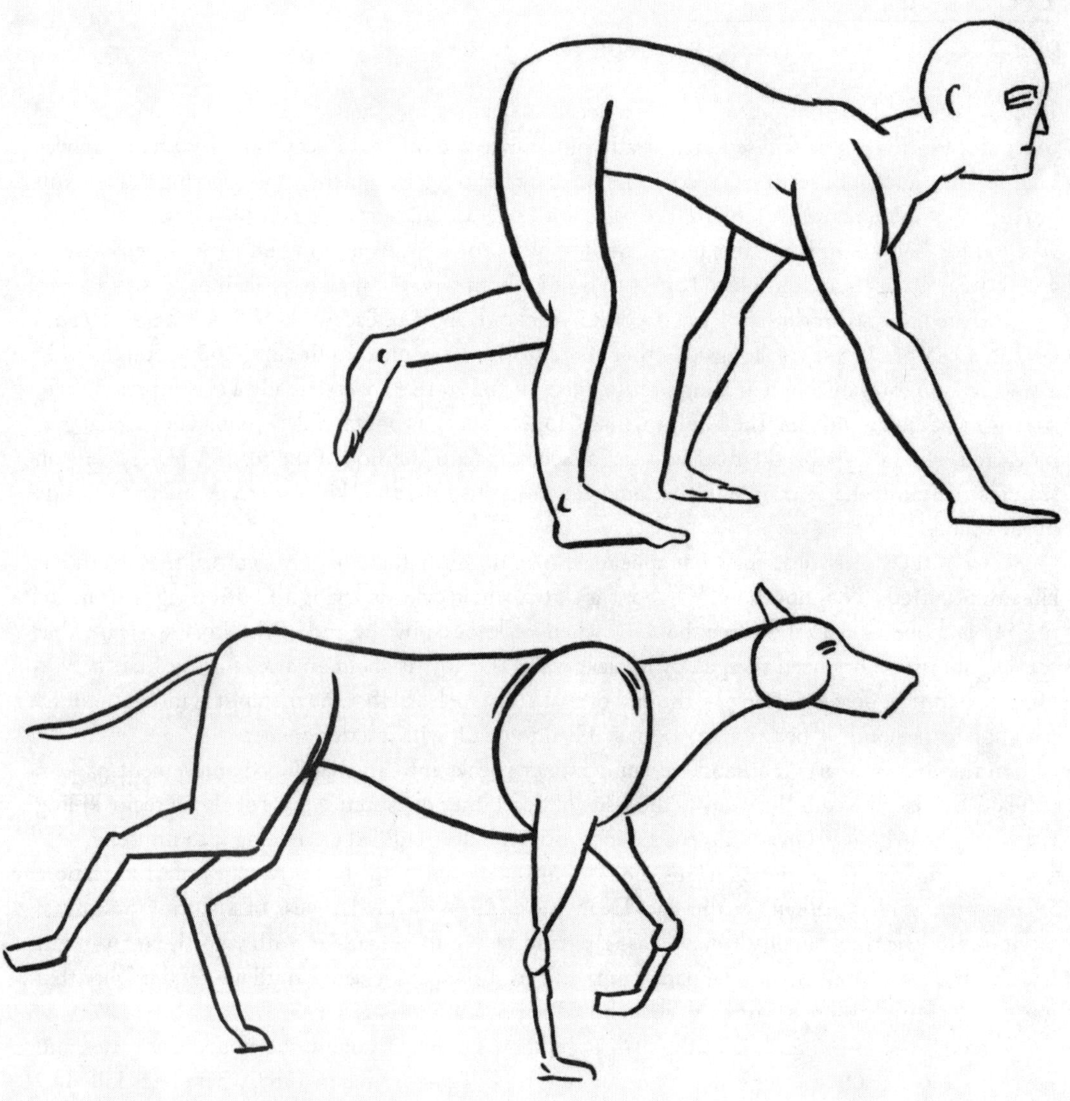

MAUREEN SELWOOD

Poem to My Dog, Monday, On Night I Accidentally Ate Meat

MAX RITVO

The lights went out on Monday
lying on a green rug -
wanting to make noise, only -

a visitation left
in his small white body.

The symbol is outrageous: like a hungry man
slamming down jam jars
in the pantry of the Viewer's soul.

Thank God for the past tense, and its order.
And that Monday died before it was symbolic.

Monday, the Hunt left your bed,
your blood-down and quilted gut.

Monday, it found a white star
in your body to sleep in.

Monday, it's leaving me too.
Monday, why does life love the stars? The famous stars?

Monday, with your millions of soft horns,
wear your barking-mad
wizard's hat
and I will slip behind your eyes,
loading myself like a cartridge of light.

I will live in your small ecstatic brain
and take your life,

and you can take mine,
and we won't give our lives to cancer,
but to each other.

And thank God for the future,
where we levitate
or maybe Oblivion curls down our ears
into wings, or figs that He eats.

ARTIST PORTFOLIO

CLARISSA TOSSIN

I WORK across video, photography, sculpture, performance, and installation to reflect on the ways the built environment embodies identity, ideology, and power. Growing up in Brasília, Brazil's master-planned modern capital, made me aware of the global circulation of images of modernity and their effects on national and international psychologies. Recently in my work, I have engaged with spaces where transnational histories of Brazil and the United States remain imprinted. For *Brasília, Cars, Pools and Other Modernities*, a 1970s VW Brasilia car, loaded with pool cleaning equipment, was brought from Brasília to Santa Monica, California, to assist in the swimming pool maintenance routine of the Strick House. Brasília's main architect, Oscar Niemeyer, designed the house concurrent with his work on the city. (He never visited the building, though, as his communist affiliations prevented him from entering the US for many years.) The installation draws parallels between the two places through architecture, car culture, and biographical recollections. Another recent body of work examines Ford's rubber plantation villages in the Brazilian Amazon and a local architectonic style, New England's Cape Cod cottage, brought to the tropical forest. As part of this body of work, the video installation *Streamlined: Belterra, Amazônia / Alberta, Michigan* contrasts Belterra, Ford's second town in the Amazon, with its "twin," Alberta, in Michigan's Upper Peninsula. In the installation, each of the two channels is projected onto either side of a freestanding wall. Each side presents just one town, but the framing, camera movements, pacing, and edits are equivalent. By *streamlining* the video editing, visual differences — such as the landscape, architectural adaptations, and each town's daily rhythm — establish a sense of place where specific cultural aspects alter these formally equivalent, preconceived urban spaces. The installation presents an uncanny situation where the corresponding cinematography makes the familiar foreign and the foreign familiar.

WHEN TWO PLACES LOOK ALIKE, 2012–2013
DIGITAL CHROMOGENIC PRINTS, 40 X 27"

WHEN TWO PLACES LOOK ALIKE, 2012–2013
DIGITAL CHROMOGENIC PRINTS, 40 X 27"

WHEN TWO PLACES LOOK ALIKE, 2012–2013
DIGITAL CHROMOGENIC PRINTS, 40 X 27"

STREAMLINED: BELTERRA, AMAZÔNIA / ALBERTA, MICHIGAN, 2013
TWO-CHANNEL HD VIDEO PROJECTIONS (15:00 MIN EACH),
EIGHT-CHANNEL SOUND INSTALLATION, BELTERRA'S WOODEN BENCH REPLICAS, AND PHOTOGRAPH

STREAMLINED: BELTERRA, AMAZÔNIA / ALBERTA, MICHIGAN, 2013
TWO-CHANNEL HD VIDEO PROJECTIONS (15:00 MIN EACH),
EIGHT-CHANNEL SOUND INSTALLATION, BELTERRA'S WOODEN BENCH REPLICAS, AND PHOTOGRAPH
INSTALLATION VIEW: MUSEUM OF LATIN AMERICAN ART, LONG BEACH, 2015
PHOTOS: BRICA WILCOX

STUDY FOR A LANDSCAPE (BRASÍLIA), 2012
ARCHIVAL INKJET PRINT, 30 X 30"
COURTESY SAMUEL FREEMAN, LOS ANGELES

STUDY FOR A LANDSCAPE (MARS), 2012
ARCHIVAL INKJET PRINT, 30 X 30"
COURTESY SAMUEL FREEMAN, LOS ANGELES

FOLLOWING SPREAD:
BRASÍLIA, CARS, POOLS AND OTHER MODERNITIES, 2009–2013
VOLKSWAGEN BRASILIA, POOL CLEANING EQUIPMENT, STRAW HAT AND FLIP-FLOPS, SINGLE-CHANNEL HD VIDEO (10:06 MIN), PHOTOGRAPHS, ALUMINUM PLAQUE REPLICA, LETTER, BOOK-PAGE INKJET TRANSFERS, DRAWING ON VELLUM PAPER, AND BOOK.
INSTALLATION VIEW: ARTPACE SAN ANTONIO, JULY 11 – SEPT. 15, 2013
ORIGINALLY COMMISSIONED AND PRODUCED BY ARTPACE SAN ANTONIO.
PHOTOS BY TODD JOHNSON.

Brasilia. O sucesso comprovado até
nos caminhos mais difíceis.

BRASÍLIA, CARS, POOLS AND OTHER MODERNITIES, 2009-2013
VOLKSWAGEN BRASILIA, POOL CLEANING EQUIPMENT, STRAW HAT AND FLIP-FLOPS,
SINGLE-CHANNEL HD VIDEO (10:06 MIN), PHOTOGRAPHS, ALUMINUM PLAQUE REPLICA,
LETTER, BOOK-PAGE INKJET TRANSFERS, DRAWING ON VELLUM PAPER, AND BOOK.
INSTALLATION VIEW: ARTPACE SAN ANTONIO, JULY 11 - SEPT. 15, 2013
ORIGINALLY COMMISSIONED AND PRODUCED BY ARTPACE SAN ANTONIO.
PHOTOS BY TODD JOHNSON.

FOLLOWING SPREAD:
TRANSPLANTED (VW BRASILIA), 2012
NATURAL LATEX, 12.5' X 9' X 7"
INSTALLATION VIEW: GALERIA LUISA STRINA, SÃO PAULO, 2014
COURTESY GALERIA LUISA STRINA, SÃO PAULO.
PHOTOS: EDOUARD FRAIPONT

MANUTENÇÃO DE
PISCINAS
9228-7806

THE APHASIA BOOK CLUB

LOUISE STEINMAN

THUS FAR, it looks like any book club: nine adults (including me) seated around a rectangular table in the humble meeting room at the Echo Park Branch of the Los Angeles Public Library. People riffle through snacks set out on the counter — edamame and string cheese, nuts, cookies, and apple juice from Trader Joe's.

Today's meeting will focus on chapters 10 and 11 of *The Lost City of Z*, David Grann's gripping nonfiction chronicle about the legendary British explorer Percy Fawcett, who in 1925 ventured into the green hell of the Amazonian rainforest on a quixotic search for a fabled civilization, and never returned.

Francie Schwarz, an effervescent librarian with curly hair and a ready laugh, is the group's facilitator. She hands out today's study questions about Fawcett's singular obsession, his nutty stoicism in the face of starvation and disease, and how he and his crew descended unmarked chutes of the Amazon — some of which dropped hundreds of feet. To get the conversation moving, she throws out a basic question, glancing at the faces around the table: "What was your favorite part of the chapter?" No one raises a hand.

She tries another approach, using the same enthusiastic tone: "If you could time-travel, where would you go?" She makes the idea sound, well, *possible*. Her own choice, she volunteers, is "the Americas before Europeans." My mental movie unspools thundering bison herds on the prairie, Chumash warriors in long boats.

"Space trav-el ..." Laura's voice breaks in, the tone flat, the syllables uninflected. Schwarz's question has jump-started the group into a more fluent reverie. Laura continues: "To see earth from above. But not ex-pensive." Expressions on faces around the table suggest responses brewing, but no one interrupts during the long pauses in Laura's sentences.

Larry — the group's elder statesman, its moral philosopher — takes up the theme. He speaks with great deliberation and considerable effort.

> Into the future, I would like to move on. [pause]
> I am always in the past,
> though I'm only two minutes [pause]
> from the future.

Some of his pauses are longer than his sentences. Everyone appears to be listening intently to Larry's gruff voice. Is this quality of attention just polite restraint? No, it's something else; something notably absent from much social exchange these days — it's *patience*.

Each person here respects the effort, the frustration of trying to locate the words, the sounds that form a sentence. After all, this is *not* an ordinary book group. This is the weekly meeting of the Aphasia Book Club, intended for those who have suffered damage to an area of the brain that affects the use of language. Larry continues:

> When I read a book, it puts me in the future,
> even when it's written in the past.

Larry's going for it. He so wants to get the words right. He leans forward in his wheelchair; grips the table with his one good hand to aid the effort:

> I see a person like myself living in the future [long pause]
> always finding a book …
> so the more I experience,
> the more future I'm living in.

Jeff — dark-haired, handsome — replies with cheerful sincerity: "Thank you! That was very weird! Thank you!"

Everyone guffaws. Then Ron volunteers that he wants to "go back to the '60s: where people did drugs, didn't think much about politics, just had a good time." I'm back at Mist Mountain Farm — our Oregon commune — a naked acid trip in the garden.

Schwarz gently asks Levander — who has perhaps the most difficulty speaking — "Where might you time-travel?" His answer is a shrug and a smile. He will not speak, but he is pleased to have been asked.

"The late 19th century, the age of invention," is Susan's choice. A few of us chime in, listing a few discoveries from that time: the telephone, escalators, the rabies vaccine.

Lastly, Uma puts her gift of time travel to good use:

> I would go to Cedars,
> And I would drill my skull.
> And I wouldn't have an aneurysm.

I've been a visitor in the Land of Aphasia for just over a year now. When I join the group around the table in the Echo Park Branch meeting room, I practice listening. I sharpen my awareness of gestural cues, facial expressions. I practice not racing ahead. I practice accepting the unsaid as part of what is said. I make note that what does get communicated is usually worth the wait. For hyper verbal me,

KERRY TRIBE, *THE LOSTE NOTE*, 2015. INSTALLATION SHOT.

attending the weekly two-hour session of the Aphasia Book Club is a welcome refuge from the daily barrage of emails, texts — my speeded-up multitasking reality. If, as poet Diane Ackerman writes, "words are the pass-key to the soul," then the communal effort to find words — as I witness in this room — is a soulful endeavor.

The members of the Aphasia Book Club are all more than a year out from their initial injury, what's called the chronic stage of aphasia. Some have more difficulty with the reception and recognition of spoken and/or written language, others with the production of speech.

Over the last several months, I've learned some details of their injuries, their backgrounds. I know that pre-stroke, Larry was a theater professional — he directed plays Off-Broadway and on; he directed TV and film and taught theater for decades. Now he's in a wheelchair, his body bowed. Under the brim of his baseball cap, however, his eyes are unmistakably inquisitive, mischievous.

Susan, a graceful woman with the cheekbones of Meryl Streep, was a yoga teacher for 20 years. She was demonstrating an asana in front of a class when she collapsed — to awake in the ICU, unable to speak or move. For many years, she has been the leader, "the boss," as she jokingly puts it, of the Cedars-Sinai Aphasia Support Group, where many of the participants in this book club first met.

Jeff, in his 40s, injured his brain in a water-skiing accident when he was 26. Fifteen days prior to his massive stroke, Dean had started his dream sales job for a solar manufacturing company. He volunteers twice a week at the homeless shelter at St. Charles Borromeo Service Center in Moorpark and attends the book club faithfully. "Reading helps with my talking," he says, "I'm doing what I gotta do." Laura was once a creative design manager at a tech company. She blacked out at home in the shower, a prelude to many smaller strokes, caused by a constriction of her internal carotid artery, a disease known as Moyamoya, Japanese for "smoke" (so named because the arteries branch out from the constriction, resembling the branches of a tree or a puff of smoke).

Uma, with family roots in Sri Lanka, suffered her stroke just a week after her fiancé (now her husband) proposed to her. She was an aspiring actor at the time, just 27. For weeks she hovered between life and death. I know this because a friend of hers wrote an excellent play based on his experience waiting outside the ICU in the days after Uma was stricken. Strokes and the consequences of aphasia change not only the lives of those who suffer them, but also the lives of spouses, lovers, parents, friends — those who care for them and those who love them.

Aphasia is talking.
No.
Because.
Speak slowly.
words
lost
lost
darn it
but
trying
trying
trying
— Chris Riley

When I first saw the phrase "Aphasia Book Club," I thought it was a joke. It was on a list of mini-grants funded by the Library Foundation of Los Angeles, the nonprofit where I work. "Aphasia" and "book club" would seem to make strange bedfellows. Or so I thought. As it turns out, it's a brilliant coupling.

Like many others, I mistakenly assumed that difficulty in speaking implied a deficit in intellectual acuity. It's not true. As Laura succinctly informed me: "Aphasia is a language problem. The core of your intelligence is totally intact." Which makes it even more heartbreaking when an adult with a full quota of life experience and intelligence is treated as if s/he has the comprehension of a toddler. Those who attend the book club have a special drive; their presence here is one way that they actively combat the social isolation and concomitant depression that often results from aphasia.

The neurologist Antonio Damasio defines aphasia (literally "without speech") as "a breakdown of the two-way translation that establishes a correspondence between thoughts and language." Most commonly, the condition is the result of a stroke caused by a blood clot or a bleed in the brain; but it can be caused by virtually any neurologic insult that affects language-related areas in the cerebral hemispheres People with aphasia have trouble speaking, reading, usually writing, too — depending on what area of the brain was injured.

The manifestation of aphasia can range from a near-complete loss of the ability to retrieve words or understand what others are saying to fairly fluent speech and a comprehension that only breaks down when language becomes more complex (with some poetry, for example). Whatever the severity of aphasia, it's a very frustrating experience, compounded by a general lack of public awareness of the condition. There are passionate advocates for AIDS, muscular dystrophy, breast cancer, and other diseases; but it's difficult to be a vocal advocate for aphasia when your speech comes out a jumble.

The idea of starting a book club for adults with aphasia was the brainchild of Francie Schwarz and her husband, Dr. Mike Biel, a speech pathologist. Schwarz, a librarian with the Los Angeles Public Library since 2011, realized that — even with the huge array of resources at the public library — aphasia sufferers were not being well served. She and Biel recruited several members from the Cedars-Sinai Aphasia Support Group to help plan the book club, which, as far as she has been able to establish, is the first and only aphasia book club at a public library in North America, perhaps in the world.

Schwarz's initial proposal met with both enthusiasm and skepticism. Her supervisor liked the idea, but public library resources must by definition be offered for free, and funds were needed for supplies like study guides from the Aphasia Center of California, audio versions of selected books, and snacks for the participants. The Library Foundation grant covered these expenses and provided the seed money to get started.

But there were other well-founded concerns about the venture. Book clubs at libraries, under the best of circumstances, can be hard to sustain. "They may start off strong," Schwarz told me, "but membership eventually dwindles to three or four people, who may or may not show up. What none of us understood, except for perhaps Mike, was that you will never find more motivated readers than those who can no longer take reading, or the ability to discuss what they've read, for granted."

Mike Biel began working with people with aphasia at the VA hospital as part of his training in speech pathology and it was there that he began his study of the disorder. For a long time, he told me, it was common for many doctors to inform their stroke patients that the "window of opportunity" for regaining mental and physical abilities closes after three months to a year. For many, this became a self-fulfilling prophecy. Biel, a tall, lean, affable man who enjoys the give-and-take of conversation, frequently reminds people that yes, aphasia is a medical condition; but it's a *treatable* medical condition.

With new research and data supporting the scientific credibility of neuroplasticity, what neurologist Oliver Sacks calls "the endless adaptability of the human brain," there is no longer an accepted "plateau" for recovering language. Use it or lose it. As Biel often reminds the group, if you keep working, if you keep practicing, if you keep trying to read and trying to speak, improvement comes. Most people with aphasia, he observes, struggle with motivation.

"What the Aphasia Book Club implicitly says," explains Biel, "is that everyone here has the intellectual capacity to read and understand books that others who have not had a stroke can understand."

Schwarz adds, "When you are talking about a really good book — or even a crappy book for that matter — there's always something in there that's going to be about you or your life or someone you know. And when that happens, the disability becomes incidental. We're just a group of people talking about this book, and often, honestly, I forget that people in the group are having trouble speaking. I'm just listening and they're saying interesting things and I'm so grateful."

The actor Kirk Douglas suffered a stroke in 1996. His memoir, *My Stroke of Luck*, is recommended on the booklist provided by the Aphasia Center of California. The last chapter is our discussion topic today.

This reading selection has not been a universal hit. Schwarz reassures everyone it's okay if they don't like the book, and that they're welcome — in the future — to depart from the vetted reading list. Everyone is buoyed by that news.

Then they're off and running. Uma loved the Douglas book. Larry hated it: "I wanted him to say something I hadn't thought of. Something new. Doesn't have enough oomph."

Dale, who, before his stroke, worked in film production, owns that Douglas is a "good guy." "But," he complains, in his inventive syntax, "he has also so above it all." Susan likewise has little sympathy for the movie star: "He got into his pity party. He name-drops a *lot*. As if he's the only one who suffered. What about *me*?"

"I am also in Vietnam. He didn't give that in there!" Dale indignantly adds. Susan has another criticism: "Little people! Thousands of us out here!" Dale sums it up, pounds his hand on the table: "We learned to THROUGH it!"

As the emotional tenor shifts down a gear, Schwarz gently queries the group, "How does surviving a stroke change you?" I think of my father — whose first heart attack struck at age 50 — confessing his terror of suffering a stroke, being left mute and helpless (like his best friend Artie Bushkin). It was the fate he feared more than any other.

What I'm hearing today, though, would have surprised him as much as it does me. After his stroke, relates Ron: "You have a second life to lead, and when you have a second life, you want to do good. And that's why people look to God. Before the stroke, you didn't have *TIME* to think about God and people who help me. Before I cared, but I really didn't do anything about it." Jeff concurs, adding: "You have *time*. Think about what you're doing. Your friends aren't what they used to be."

Something *is* lost, but what I begin to understand is that there are unique gifts bestowed by this disability as well. In this reordered way of thinking and speaking, something is gained. Ron reminds us, "It's not easy. Are you going to work on it. Or not?" After a silence, Uma says, "I love our book group. I love everyone here."

With aphasia, sometimes the right word finds its way to the surface. Often it doesn't. Sometimes the brain takes a scenic byway. Then, the "wrong" word may serve as the right word. "Frog" becomes "fork." "Volcano" gains a syllable — "volacano." For those of us in the room who are nonaphasic, the instinct to help — that is, to jump in — is difficult to suppress.

Schwarz poses that question to the whole group: "When is it appropriate for me to say what I think you're trying to say?"

Jeff has a ready answer: "I say 'one,' but means 'two.' When my mother tries to jump in and correct," he grins, "I tell her, 'Shhhh … you might learn something!'"

While a few of us nod in recognition of a truth, Susan jumps in. "I may say yes when I mean no," she says. "But I know the difference. I'm trying." This inspires Larry, who says, in a gruff voice: "When you say yes when I mean no, it's a way of erasing me as a person. If you [pointing to Schwarz, whose eyes open wide] correct me, I'm grateful. If a stranger does it, and they're wrong, then I'm angry."

Again we wait in silence — some of us contemplating the times we might have gotten it wrong. Susan adds: "Good to wait. Let us find another word. Like looking for a parking spot. When you get too many suggestions, your brain gets confused. Everyone has to rush."

Biel explains how words that are "high frequency" are easier for people with aphasia to say. "Imagine all the words in our head are on the bottom of the ocean," he says, "and we have to activate them with our brain. It's harder to find words you didn't use before."

One word few people here used before their stroke is *aphasia*. It's hard to remember. It's hard to pronounce. It's buried under rocks at the bottom of the sea.

"Let's rebrand aphasia!" Susan suggests with a subversive glint in her eye.

"Acquired word loss?" suggests Schwarz, helpfully. There's a collective good-natured groan, then Jeff grins. "Let's call it 'Bob,'" he says. No silence then, just a roomful of laughing.

The nature of the insult that results in aphasia is a blockage of blood to the affected region of the brain causing a lesion, a death of cells. The location of the dead cells pinpoints the functions concentrated in that area, allowing researchers insight into the location of the processes of the mind. In the brain, function is in part ascribed to location. As my neurologist brother, Dr. Lawrence Steinman, explained, "You can't recreate the situation that occurs in a stroke with an experimental subject in a lab. We study strokes resulting in aphasia because it informs us most eloquently about the location in the brain of the most human of functions — language."

Psychologists, linguists, computational scientists, and philosophers are also drawn to study aphasia as a testing ground for theories of mind and brain. So are artists. The Aphasia Book Club also served as a laboratory of sorts for Kerry Tribe, a Los Angeles–based visual artist whose work in film, video, and installation probes the gaps between perception, cognition, and memory.

Tribe began her recent project over a year ago by "embedding" at the Cedars-Sinai Aphasia Support Group. She spent hundreds of hours recording interviews, eventually narrowing her subjects to three — Dale, Laura, and another stroke patient, Chris Riley. Their intertwined narratives became the subject of a film, a 28-minute loop, that was the centerpiece of Tribe's provocative installation *The Loste Note*, which ran this past spring at 356 Mission in downtown Los Angeles.

I met Tribe, an energetic and enthusiastic woman in her early 40s, at the book club on a hot afternoon last summer. She wore shorts and sandals, her long hair loose. She'd brought a big bag of fresh plums from her backyard in Eagle Rock to add to the array of snacks. I noticed right away her easy familiarity with the group members, and they with her.

That day she screened some footage from her film-in-progress to the group, prompting Ron to ask, "What do you think the audience will get out of this?"

"I want people to understand what people with aphasia struggle with," she told him. "I want to create an aphasic space for a nonaphasic audience."

When I visited her Glendale studio not long after, Tribe was still unsure of how to structure the narrative. We sipped from mugs of dark tea as she brooded aloud on how paradoxical it was to make a documentary featuring "people talking about having a hard time talking."

Six months later, when I finally saw the finished version of *The Loste Note*, Tribe's three-channel film installation, I was astonished. She had completely abandoned the idea of pictorially representing her subjects. You will see no faces of the subjects in Tribe's "documentary." Instead, she forged a cinematic language to convey her subjects' inner experiences, their attempts to reconstruct the past, their meditations on how they inhabit the present moment.

The Loste Note is an experiment in radical empathy; empathy in the sense that essayist Leslie Jamison defines as "a penetration, a kind of travel. It suggests you enter another person's pain as you'd enter another country, through immigration and customs, border crossing by way of query." Using imagery, animation, and editing, Tribe's installation asks the question, "What does it feel like to live in the Land of Aphasia?"

A viewer watches intercut images of architectural interiors, wind-blown green jungle palms, shooting stars, tangles of arteries viewed through a microscope, glistening geological specimens. We hear Laura's voice recounting the morning of her stroke, how she fell into a bush, "not knowing it was crooked," while on-screen the interior courtyard of a mid-century apartment collapses in on itself and the landscape shifts to a precarious tilt. When asked by her speech therapist to name fruits, Laura can only — bizarrely — come up with the word "star fruit." An armada of gorgeous golden star fruits blazes right to left across the three screens. Who could ever forget a starfruit?

Chris Riley, one of the three subjects in the film, was an accomplished artist before his stroke. As a young photographer, he and another photographer, Douglas Niven, traveled to Phnom Penh, Cambodia, where, on the second floor of an old schoolhouse — the notorious Tuol Sleng, which became known by the shorthand S-21 — they discovered rusting metal cases containing over 7,000 decaying photo negatives. This was the discarded "official" archive of the Khmer Rouge — the faces of startled victims posing before their executions. Riley and Niven took on the arduous job of restoring the negatives, and, in 1996, published the photos as a book (*The Killing Fields*, Twin Palms Publishers). Their project, exhibited at MOMA, is a unique and extraordinarily harrowing record of a genocide.

Chris's scratchy nasal post-stroke voice yields hauntingly beautiful jumbled text in the film, his sentences set against black-and-white images of the killing fields, then sparkling orange then yellow then lavender geological specimens, galaxies bursting open, his artist's sense of wonder undeniably intact:

I collect rocks.
I collect meteorites.
I collect rocks
and meteorites
and crystals.
I am a
pho tog raphcr.
Now
I turn
and capture
negatives upside down
upside down is
upside down is
is here. This.

Brain?
Molecules.

Molecules.
Billions!
Billions!
Atoms spilling.
Speaking and
thinking and thinking
and space.
Wow!
Stars!
Wow!
Sun!
But
concentrate
concentrate.
Keep talking.
Oh
then,
wow!
Wow!
Amazing!

Dale's inside-out sentences recounting his traumatic four years in Vietnam as a Navy SEAL are voiced by his avatar, an (animated) seal sporting a red kerchief and a white sailor cap. The creature's mien is mournful, even remorseful, as he explains one source of his memory misery:

And … he died because I had to koot him first
for he was going to kill me first.
I haven't been able to put that out back of my brain …

Before his injury, Dale had been on a decades-long quest to make an animated children's film. After his stroke, however, none of his former film industry colleagues would take him seriously. Tribe creates her own version of Dale's unmade film, in an ecstatic finale where a magical animated kingdom bursts into life with a smiling "Volacano" presiding over a world of "buttleflies" and bees and buds (bugs), and a beneficent spider (or "spidder," in Dale-speak) conducts a rousing chorus sung by all the creatures. The song (which stuck in my head for weeks) celebrates a new-forged bond among friends who understand each other, who come together to read poetry and books — in short, the Aphasia Book Club.

Previously, Tribe and I had attended a book club session that tackled Stanley Kunitz's magnificent poem "The Layers." We took turns reading the lines aloud:

I have walked through many lives,
some of them my own,
and I am not who I was,
though some principle of being
abides, from which I struggle
not to stray.
When I look behind,
as I am compelled to look
before I can gather strength
to proceed on my journey,
I see the milestones dwindling
toward the horizon
and the slow fires trailing
from the abandoned camp-sites,
over which scavenger angels
wheel on heavy wings.
Oh, I have made myself a tribe
out of my true affections,
and my tribe is scattered!
How shall the heart be reconciled
to its feast of losses?

As I listened, I pondered the "feast of losses" present in the room. Careers dashed, plans waylaid, self-images upended. As different members read aloud, they transformed words into other words, making surprising cognitive substitutions.

The poem ends, some lines later, on the poet's "darkest night," during which he hears a "nimbus clouded voice" that directs him to "Live in the layers, / not on the litter."

"Does anyone want to respond?" asked Schwarz. A long silence; two people held their heads in their hands.

Dale was the first to speak, admitting he felt "lost." Ron said the poem made him dizzy. Uma added, "In listening, I went and closed my eyes."

With aphasia, the brain's ability to generate meaning to match a sentence that is heard or read is often impaired. In Tribe's film, we hear Laura's voice describe how — in spite of that disability — she found her own work-around to ultimately absorb Kunitz's poem:

And it's beautiful but I don't hear it so
I just see everyone and can feel it in my gut
but I can't really hear it so I just feel everyone's warmth
and emotion and then it's abstract, it's not a narrative
that makes sense. So then I got to the point where
he says "live in the layers" and I cried.

Laura's words gather themselves like a poem, recalling Tribe's belief that "in a sense, all poets have aphasia. They are always struggling to find the right word." Poets and people with aphasia share the gift of altered perception.

One Saturday I meet for coffee with Susan Swan, the yoga teacher, to talk about her stroke, to hear her tell how she had to start all over again learning to speak, to understand speech. She tells me how, when she first heard about it, she also thought the Aphasia Book Club was a joke. ("Me too. I was hahaha ...") She attests to how attending the Aphasia Book Club and pushing herself to try what seemed impossible helped her regain the ability to read fluently.

"You never know where your next teacher will come from," she told me calmly, referring to her stroke. One of the lessons of her stroke experience was the realization of how "so much of what we talk about is useless, to fill up space." While still in the hospital, she recalled, a friend came to visit. He sat on the edge of her bed and kept chattering, "What are you going to do? What are you going to do? What are you going to do ...??"

"I looked at him," she said, "and told him, '*I'm going to go on.*'"

"I can't go on, I'll go on." The famous line from Samuel Beckett, who in *Waiting for Godot* describes God's inscrutability as "divine aphasia" and whose protagonist in the novel *Watt* jumbles the order of words and their meanings. Near the end of his life, Beckett himself suffered a stroke and experienced the torments and isolation of aphasia, no longer able to render in words and sentences the thoughts in his head.

I've continued attending the Aphasia Book Club long past that first visit, the one based on sheer curiosity. The group members have ventured far afield from the approved "aphasia-friendly" reading syllabus.

Last fall, they spent weeks reading my 2001 memoir, *The Souvenir*, based on my father's letters home from the Pacific War and, as well, my return of a Japanese flag to the family of a Japanese soldier my father faced in battle. Growing up in a permissive household, my siblings and I were issued one strong admonition: "Never ask your father to talk about the war." It was a silence that informed my childhood, and one I sought to unravel after my father's sudden death from a heart attack in 1990. Cleaning out my parents' condo, I discovered a metal box with over 400 letters that my father wrote home to my mother from the Philippines, where he served in the US Infantry. He'd endured, I learned, a gruesome battle that lasted over 165 consecutive days. In the letters, I encountered the expressive poetic man my father had been before the war, before combat took its toll.

Reading *The Souvenir* spurred conversations around the table about the invisible wounds of war, about family secrets, about living with someone who has been altered by trauma. Uma talked about her family's exodus from Sri Lanka after the civil war there, how no one in her family would talk about it. "Like a curtain came down," she said. Dale saw "awful things" as a Navy SEAL in Vietnam, but could not or would not say more because a Navy SEAL has to be, in his words, "silent on top of silent." Laura, adopted as an infant from Korea, remembered when a Korean War vet called her a "bad word," and she had to ask her dad about it. Dean was inspired by reading the book to query his mother, who'd kept the letters of his grandfather, who was stationed at Pearl Harbor during World War II. Larry told me, "Your book would make a good film," and added wistfully, " I wish I could direct it."

Next up, Uma suggested that we read a play, and Larry cast his vote for Clifford Odets's gritty 1935 family drama, *Awake and Sing!*, which the author described as "a struggle for life amidst petty conditions." Years ago, Larry directed the play Off-Broadway. The book club members asked him to lead the discussion. Larry's wife, April, an accomplished actor and acting teacher, joined our session that day. She reminded the group how in a novel the narrator can tell you everything. "But in a play, it is the actor and director who give meaning to the words." I sensed she was nervous for Larry in his role as discussion leader.

Larry had a lesson plan in mind for our session. He'd haltingly read a sentence aloud, then demand, "What does that MEAN?" With new authority, he looked directly at each one of us in turn. His voice grew stronger, his gaze bold. In the playwright's introduction, Odets describes the character of the Jewish mother as both "naïve and quick [...] afraid of utter poverty." Larry asked, "What is naïveté?" "People who are not reflective?" ventured Laura. "Yes, *that's* the difference!" said Larry. "Isn't the mother both shrewd *and* naive?" Susan suggested. "Yes," said Larry. "Every mistake in her life leads to right wrong." *Shrewd. Naive.* More words uncovered from the bottom of the ocean, more precise syllables to give color to inner experiences. Parsing the characters and their motivations fascinated everyone, as we encountered aspects of our own flaws, values, habits, quirks. I glanced at Larry's wife. She was beaming.

Speaking to the audience at a panel discussion after the opening of Kerry Tribe's exhibit, Larry explained what the Aphasia Book Club has meant to him:

> I've spent more time in this group than I've been in any club,
> because the ones that would have me — I wouldn't want to be with.
> [pause]
> So I came to this group moaning and groaning,
> and I learned so much in the group. [pause]
>
> I learned so much from other people.
>
> This deserves me to be part of it. I did. And I am.
> And I still do feel a part of it.
> And I want to thank those who organized the group [pause]
> for enriching my life, really enriching it [pause]
> more than I ever thought possible [pause]
>
> [he gestures to his mouth]
>
> When I lost my tongue.

RISKING PERFECTION

ALISSA WILKINSON

I WAS ALWAYS one of the tall kids, but the summer before I turned 12, I suddenly gained five extra inches of height. And braces. You can see it in the pictures, how I became gawky and uncomfortable, like a teenaged chicken. I hated it. My parents started having serious discussions with me about how it was a great gift and responsibility to be a woman, and at church I learned that my form was dangerous and needed to be disguised. People should appreciate me for my mind, my personality — not for my body.

But behind the braces and my discomfort, I was developing curves and gams. My long blond hair fell down my back. I was newly aware of being looked at. I liked being noticed, but it scared me, too, since it sometimes came with admonitions from adults at church who'd never spoken to me before. I hid myself in a droopy hand-me-down knit turtleneck — but it was deemed too form-fitting. I was ashamed. I understood that people would know my character from what I put on my body for the rest of my life. I took to sewing and wearing long, boxy calico jumpers.

Around this time, trolling through the shelves of VHS tapes at the local library for something to watch on a Friday night, I stumbled across a videotape of an American Ballet Theatre production of *Swan Lake*. As I watched that evening, I felt cleansed and transformed. In the world of the ballet, anyway, everything was beautiful and safe.

I'd studied ballet from ages three to 10 and then dropped it for lack of interest, but now I was fascinated. *Swan Lake* is a tragedy, of course, but even the evil black swan dances her fiery seduction with perfect poise and marvelous control. I felt elegant just watching. I sat up straighter.

When I returned the film, I checked out another — this time, *Coppélia*, the story of a doll who comes to life. After that I started dancing around the kitchen when nobody was looking, extending my foot in *tendu* or raising my arms into fifth position to the popping of the corn in the microwave.

Over the next month or two, I checked out every book about ballet in the children's section of the library. *A Very Young Dancer* was one I borrowed repeatedly. In it, photographer Jill Krementz captured a year in the life of Stephanie, a 10-year-old student at the School of American Ballet in 1976. I learned that the school was connected to the famous New York City Ballet, and that Stephanie lived on Manhattan's Upper East Side with her family, a long way from my house in upstate New York. Stephanie loved horses and dancing, and, in the book, she was cast as Marie, the lead child's role, in *The Nutcracker*. The pages were filled with black-and-white photographs —

portraits of Stephanie with big eyes, long dark hair, gripping the barre, doing her homework, dancing at Lincoln Center; she looked pretty normal except for her tightly pinned bun. Like hundreds of other girls, I suppose, I mentally pasted my face over hers, imagining myself as the girl in the studio, at the desk, on stage in a beautiful dress. But I was invisible — unless I was wearing or doing something wrong.

My aunt took me to the Saratoga Performing Arts Center that summer, where New York City Ballet Company spends the month of July. We saw *Swan Lake*, and I sat riveted in the amphitheater, the thick humid summer night air on my skin, crickets singing through the act breaks, the costumes and lights and sets so vivid I didn't want to turn my head for a moment.

Ballet worships the female form, lithe and strong. Today, at companies like New York City Ballet, a dancer must be slender, flat-chested, long-legged, and long-muscled. Because she has to be partnered by a man, she can't be too heavy, too muscular, or too tall on pointe; and for George Balanchine (City Ballet's late founder and choreographer), she'd better not be too curvy. Her skin should be taut and flawless, hair swept off the face and pulled back tightly, exposing her bone structure and expressive eyes. In short: the professional female dancer — the very embodiment of beauty and grace — is a lovelier and more sinewy version of a teenage boy. On stage, anyway, it is not a ballerina's breasts, or hips, or flowing hair, or any of the usual signifiers that lend her femininity. Rather, it's about what her body can *do*: its gracefulness, its shyness, its ability to bend.

At 13, at the Saratoga Performing Arts Center, I watched the prima ballerina dance both parts — the white and black swans — feathers covering her torso, a tutu floating around her. She arched her back in one smooth rolling line; she danced without fear or shame; she exulted in the applause and the music.

I felt I could be happy, if only I could be *that*.

Balanchine's most famous ballet does not star a woman: it features a girl, a prepubescent child. For each performance during *Nutcracker* season, which stretches roughly from Thanksgiving to New Year's, the cavernous theater at Lincoln Center crowds with kids — little boys in ties and vests, and girls in velvet dresses — who prop themselves on the edges of their seats, chattering excitedly, peering at the stage to see what will happen next.

The traditional *Nutcracker* staging is simple and lighthearted, easy for children to enjoy. The curtain rises on a Christmas party at the home of Marie, a sweet little girl, and Fritz, her rambunctious younger brother. Along with all the other child guests, they are wound up by the holiday, by sweets and presents. The adults stand by, bemusedly watching and drinking wine, until mysterious old Drosselmeier, Marie's godfather, arrives with his nephew, who is a little older and more serious than the rest of the children. The eccentric old magician performs tricks for the crowd and introduces Marie to his nephew, who shakes her hand. Drosselmeier also gives her a gift: a Nutcracker doll, which Fritz promptly steals and breaks. The old man ties a bandage around the doll, Fritz is scolded for his mischief, and the children and adults dance — Marie with Drosselmeier's well-mannered nephew.

When the last guest has left, Marie, in her nightdress, curls up on the couch near the Christmas tree and falls asleep with the still-bandaged Nutcracker in her arms. Not much time passes before she awakes to discover giant mice running into the room. If this isn't terrifying enough, there's more:

the Christmas tree is growing, and growing, and growing, until it is so big that neither Marie nor the audience can see the top. Fritz's toy soldiers have grown, too, as has the Nutcracker, who leads them into battle against the mice and their seven-headed King. With Marie's help, the Nutcracker slays the Mouse King with his sword, and is transformed from an ugly Nutcracker to a handsome prince, who looks suspiciously like Drosselmeier's nephew.

In the second act, the prince and Marie arrive at the Land of the Sweets, where the Sugarplum Fairy and her Cavalier greet them. The prince tells his story to all; then the children are helped up to a throne high above the stage, where they become the audience, watching for the entire act as the sweets perform for them in turn — marzipan, hot cocoa, candy canes, tea, and more. Finally, the Sugarplum Fairy and the Cavalier return and dance a full four-part *pas de deux* — duet, solo, solo, duet — for the children. Marie, like all the little girls in the audience, sits rapt: the Sugarplum Fairy is always danced by high-ranking ballerina in the company — so for the child dancer sitting on the throne, she is more than just a role model; she is a glimpse of the girl's future, a living dream come true, especially since the Fairy herself has probably studied at SAB, maybe even with some of the same instructors.

There are of course many differences between the still-inexperienced Marie and the principal dancing the Sugarplum Fairy, but one especially stands out: the child dances in soft canvas slippers, while the woman wears the inflexible hard-tipped shoes that encase the foot and enable a dancer to literally twirl on the tips of her toes.

Going *en pointe* is a rite of passage for female dancers, the moment when the shift from girl to woman happens. The dancer's body must be strong enough to handle the stress; a child's supple bone and muscle structure can be permanently damaged if she makes the shift too soon. And when the girl is finally permitted to strap on her first pair of pointe shoes, her access to actually dancing on pointe is tightly controlled. She practices *relevé* and *bourrée* for mere minutes at first, clinging to the barre for support until she's developed the requisite stamina and skill.

This is all because dancing *en pointe* is wildly unnatural. I have run half-marathons and contorted myself in yoga class, but nothing has ever felt as strange to my body — to dance and balance and turn on one's toes requires the feet, normally at a 90-degree angle to the calves, to be fully extended, as if they were a part of the leg. The dancer must effectively break the natural curve of her skeleton to make them straight, and the soles of the shoes as well as the toes are strictly reinforced to help distribute the dancer's weight.

Every young dancer anticipates the day she finally starts pointe — and yet everyone knows that nobody can dance that way injury-free. The list of problems common to ballerinas reads like a bit of Shel Silverstein poetry, from blisters and bunionettes to neuromas, sesamoiditis, and tendonitis — never mind what can happen if a dancer slips and falls. Dancers' feet are often hopelessly warped, knotted, and old before their time.

Yet the whole idea behind dancing on pointe is for the dancer to appear to be floating, like a fairy or a swan. The illusion contrasts sharply with the pain, something the dancer must learn to grow past, and not to let show on her face or in her posture. It is the "aestheticization" of a kind of torture; a ballerina trains her body to look airy, light as breath, while ignoring what is really going on. Preserving the illusion of ease, of perfection, of effortless weightlessness, is key.

Balanchine patterned his *Nutcracker* after the original choreography that he himself had danced as a young man in Russia. It premiered in New York in 1954, and one has to wonder if the audience then — a crowd of cultured cosmopolitans at the height of psychoanalysis's reign — would have missed the undertones of sublimated longing.

For while the original E. T. A. Hoffmann fairy tale from 1816 was about the line between the real and the imagined, the ballet, quite pointedly, is about subconscious desire as it surfaces in dreams. And not just any old desires, but (perhaps daringly) the sexual urges of a girl, edging toward maturity, who, on meeting a boy at a Christmas party, feels something new stirring inside her. The jumbled emotions are focused on the injured Nutcracker doll, who turns out to be a safe bet — her protector, her prince. While the ballet sidesteps any overt expression of romance, the 1993 filmed version (in which Macaulay Culkin danced the prince/Nutcracker role) has Marie wearing a floaty white veil, very like a wedding veil, throughout the second act.

Not that dreaming of romance, prompted by fairy tales and dolls and Disney and dress-up, isn't something every 10-year-old girl is encouraged to do. But there is something about Marie's dream that stretches just beyond a little girl's idea of "happily ever after": she's not some innocent girl who thinks only of her Christmas toys. She's not interested in a faceless fantasy. In her dream, she is carried off by a very specific prince, one whom she'd met earlier that evening, and had loved and cared for by proxy in her injured Nutcracker doll.

And consider the performances by the sweets in the second act: the most significant of these is Coffee's "Arabian Dance." Delivered in an uncharacteristically midriff-baring, tutu-free costume, the choreography is undeniably seductive, as is the musical accompaniment — were we not at the ballet, we'd be watching a belly dance. In the film, NYCB principal dancer Wendy Whelan plays Coffee with a come-hither expression; the dance ends with a full split, then a roll on the floor, then a quick crawl toward the camera before she settles in a prone position, chin propped in her hands, legs lifted behind her.

Most of the other dances stay out of the realm of the sensual, but Coffee's performance, underlined by the clearly romantic *pas de deux* between the Sugarplum Fairy and the Cavalier, hints that Marie's dreams are not child's play. She is walking the line between girl and womanhood — as is the student ballerina playing the role. In character, Marie is helped into a sleigh by her Nutcracker prince, and lifted out of her dream. Would that any rite of passage were that easy — and beautiful — in real life.

In the opening scene of the balletic nightmare film *Black Swan*, pointe shoes pound across the floor in patterns divorced from bodies or faces. Nina, played by Natalie Portman, is a soloist at a prestigious New York company — a girl's soul trapped in a woman's body. To quiet the resulting madness, she dances with exquisite, cramped precision — channels herself into precisely executing the steps of the dance.

The rakish French ballet master announces the pending production of a new version of *Swan Lake* — stripped down, "visceral and real." His former muse is past her prime, and he's seeking a new swan queen. At the auditions, Nina perfectly dances the innocent white swan, Odette. But she can't muster the fire, passion, and release to embody Odile, her dark counterpart. Her repression winds up having both physical and emotional consequences. She can't let go — not in the part, and not in her life. If she does, she risks perfection. Instead, she loses weight, grinds her teeth, picks at her fingernails, and watches the rash on her back getting worse (or are feathers trying to break through the skin?). She hears voices, wings flapping, and sees phantom faces in the woodwork.

I left the theater sweating. *Black Swan* made me remember my own struggle against my body. Nina (and Natalie, too) could bare her shoulders and legs in a leotard and tights without shame, while at my worst, I had hidden my shape. But I, too, had numbed my body into submission — I remembered that feeling. Every muscle fiber in my body remembered.

By the time I started college, my obsession with ballet had subsided, taking a backseat to music and grades. I was on a campus where men outnumbered women three to one, and the girls covered themselves in baggy jeans and hooded sweatshirts. I followed suit: the only legitimate reason for a girl to stand out — the only one that wouldn't elicit whistles and comments from everyone else — was for her brains.

It was easy enough to adopt the campus uniform. But the transition to college life was otherwise difficult: I was worn down by the pressure of having to get perfect grades to prove my worth, coupled with the necessity of teaching piano, which I hated, for 15 or 20 hours a week to pay for tuition. My response to the pressure was to stop laughing, stop feeling, to become a brain on a stick. My body no longer registered "hunger" or "joy" or "pain." All I felt was sameness. I was thin, brittle, and exhausted.

Something threatened to break through, though — something my self-twisted faith had taught me to fear, something I'd meant to dodge in the shapeless clothes I'd been wearing for years.

I saw a boy I'd known since high school — a tall boy with a ready smile and green eyes. A week after my 18th birthday, he gave me a CD mix as a gift, and a hug. A sensation went straight through the center of my chest, like a drill: sharp and persistent, making me feel light-headed and frightened.

Each time I saw him, my nerves got worse, and afterward I'd shake/shiver all over, find a bathroom stall and stand there holding my breath, willing my body to stop, stop, stop, and be still. My stomach began rejecting food entirely. I'd force it down, and my stomach would force it back up. I couldn't sleep at night. I became half machine, working on autopilot, living in my mind and in the classrooms, working and not thinking about the fact that I was feeling in my body something I wasn't ready to accept, something I didn't know how to navigate.

Eventually, after months of no sleep, little food, a slow carving away of my self, one night I felt something crack. The boy told me he loved me. We were standing outside, on a staircase, in the cold. He said it was okay that I was shaking and crying. He put his arms around me, and he kissed me.

And he kept coming back. He said I was pretty and coaxed me to eat. He took me to the ballet in Saratoga. I bought a skirt to wear. One day that summer, on vacation with my family at the ocean, I sat on a bench on the boardwalk, feeling the salt on my skin and watching the teenage couples walking by and thinking, *I want that*. By the time I returned to school in the fall, I could feel the contours of my shape again. I still slept poorly and pushed myself far beyond what my body could sustain. But I let the boy touch my back, my arms, my waist. I poured myself into my homework, lived in my head and my classrooms, but once in a while, at parties, we danced. I felt my bones start to disappear beneath my skin.

Not every little girl who gets to play Marie in *The Nutcracker* makes it to pointe and, subsequently, to the City Ballet stage. The spots are limited, and the competition is fierce. Stephanie did not get to become the Sugarplum Fairy. Only a few years after *A Very Young Dancer* was released, the school administration "recommended" she leave: she spent years in turmoil, bouncing back and forth between jobs, living at a monastery, trying to get her life on track. Eventually she married and moved to Montana, where she attends an evangelical church and raises and trains horses to be graceful and obedient and strong.

But even when the child's dance dream comes true, it can only last so long — most ballerinas retire around age 40, if they're not forced out of the business earlier. Sometimes, as in Darren Aronofsky's *Black Swan*, the dream becomes a nightmare. Dance lore is rife with stories of exploitation and heartache; of careers cut short; of bodies rebelling against years of precise and relentless training. Ballet is a demanding and controlling art; some manage to keep it in check, but it can also attract those who already tend toward obsession.

For still others, the concentration required is a clarifying force. It roots the mental in the physical; focus channeled into bones, blood, and flesh, and if the body is a curse to be borne, it can offer salvation.

In the fall of my third year of college, I went back to the barre. I had encountered a challenge I couldn't surmount, in the form of a propositional logic class that finally exhausted my intellectual resources. I'd studied the rules and learned them by heart, but try as I might, I could never get from the proposition to the final proof. One night, up late studying, I felt myself hallucinate: the forms on the page became letters, and I felt sudden terror that they were a message from beyond. I stared for a solid few minutes — I don't know how long — trying to decipher the code; and then something snapped. A voice in my head said, *You're going to go nuts.*

The next day I walked to the campus fitness center and signed up for ballet classes. Two days later, a package arrived in the mail containing two leotards, two pairs of tights, a filmy wrap skirt, and a pair of soft pink canvas slippers. I opened the box in my room and put on the forest green leotard. I looked intently at myself in the mirror — my bared shoulders, my clavicle, my arms and legs: was I ready for this? I wrapped the skirt around my waist and sat down to sew the elastics onto the shoes in a crisscross pattern.

At the first class, wearing the skirt and a sweater over the leotard, I took a place in the back of the room. The teacher was young and pretty, with her hair pulled into a bun, wearing yoga pants and a spaghetti-strap top. She called out instructions, and I grasped the barre, surprised how many of the movements were still lodged in my memory and my muscles. *And prepare … plié, relevé, tendu, and close. Plié, relevé, tendu, and close …*

Every so often, when I was out of sync with the girl in front of me, I could see my own leg in the glass, darting out behind hers. I extended my foot fully and felt a twinge in the arch. I rolled my shoulders backward, pulled myself up straight, and raised my eyes again: I saw my body; I saw myself.

TATIANA WILLS
LILY TUTU

Eggs JOHN STINTZI

WIL GAVE ME a loop of keys — to every room in the house — and a large blue egg. Wil, drunk, was going on a beer run. He'd been carrying the egg around all day to display his gentleness. He said, "Don't lose my egg, and don't go into my Man Cave. But you can go anywhere else, what do I care? Show yourself around."

This was an exercise in trust. He said if I betrayed him he'd be "right miffed." He had rage problems. So did I. We met in Anger Management class, when we were learning how to yell nice things. Partnered, he yelled *YOU'RE THE PRETTIEST GIRL I'VE EVER SEEN*, and I yelled *I FUCKING LOVE YOUR EYES*. When we necked, on our third date, we used too many teeth.

I didn't go into his Man Cave, but I *almost* did. There were so many keys, so many tumbling locks. I'd never been to his place before. I wondered, after surveying the other bland rooms — an empty indoor pool, a dusty library, an abandoned yoga studio — how would he find out if I went in? Plus, we'd been taking the Anger Management class, so he *should* be tested. Our Mildness Master told us, "The world will test you every day," and on our eighth date, Wil said, "Sonja, you're my world." He should trust me even if I'm untrustworthy.

I'll admit it: I was sloshed and angry about the rules. I swaggered down the halls, leaving every door wide open out of spite, Wil's egg loosely grasped in hand. I had a little sit-down on the floor when I finally got to the Man Cave's door. It was steel, spinning, with a poster of Brett Favre on it. Bleuch. I was always a Vikings fan.

I stood, fumbled for the key on the loop, and dropped the egg. It cracked perfectly around the middle, but didn't spill. "Shit," I said, drooping. Wil was on his way. I'd gotten his text: "incoming!" He can't be angry, I rationalized, cradling the ooze, because, semantics: I didn't *lose* the egg, it broke.

So I went to the kitchen to make Wil an omelet of it. Projecting to displace the rage. The room swam. There was a slasher film on the TV inset in the fridge door: a woman was getting butchered up. I changed it to cartoons: Dexter was yelling at Dee Dee to get out of his laboratory. I practiced calm breathing. The Man Cave unhinged in my mind. The pan spat as I slid us in, the two-yolked egg.

Then, a crash. Wil ran over his bike while parking. He stumbled into the kitchen, Budweiser under arm, polishing off a road beer. This was before AA. "How do you like your eggs?" I asked. He stared at me, eyes drooping, his shoulders asway. "I'm watching my cholesterol," he said, and my calm breathing funked, because he never *did* fucking appreciate me.

So I picked up the pan and threw.

SCARLET LETTERS:
HOW NORMAN MAILER BLURRED THE LINE BETWEEN THE LURID AND THE LITERARY

ASHLEY RINDSBERG

AS A RULE, literary reputations are in a constant state of ebb and flow — in 1941 F. Scott Fitzgerald was widely thought to have died sadly unrealized, while some of the most celebrated writers of only a few years ago are today all but forgotten. But when it comes to the topic of Norman Mailer, we're faced with a reputation that's especially volatile. It's as if we don't quite know what to make of a writer whose boundless potential once seemed destined to usher in a new era of American letters but whose body of work was mixed. The result is that Mailer's legacy has been kept on a kind of literary life support as we, the next of kin, continue to argue.

Perhaps the turmoil Mailer created in his lifetime needed to be followed by a dust-settling period of relative stillness; but silence was never Mailer's thing, and so it should come as no surprise that nearly a decade after his death the question of Mailer's legacy still causes so much literary pot-banging.

When Mailer died in 2007, British novelist Joan Smith lobbed the first grenade; she spoke for many feminist writers when she penned a piece for *The Guardian* bidding "farewell" — in the title of the piece — to a "sexist, homophobic reactionary." In a 2013 piece for *The Guardian*, media gadfly Michael Wolff argued, not quite successfully, just how irrelevant Mailer is today, writing, "Mailer was a sleazeball. Not just for his unreconstructed sexual adventurism, but for his manic pursuit of glamour, attention, and dough." The most recent Mailer-related flare-up occurred when a new edition of his collected letters was released last winter. Just a year before that, J. Michael Lennon's massive, authoritative biography, *Norman Mailer: A Double Life*, was released, prompting its own round of Mailerian soul-searching. In a review of the book for *The New York Times*, Graydon Carter grasped at the meaning of "a novelist of enormous and singular narrative inventiveness and thrust" yet who "produced no single volume that captured and continues to capture the hearts and minds of successive generations"; British film critic Philip French entombed Mailer in *The Guardian* as a "Whitmanesque sage and unofficial guardian of the national conscience"; *The New York Review of Books* compared Mailer's writing "with the prophetic depth and precise observation of Tocqueville"; and across the pond, in the *London Review of Books*, Andrew O'Hagan tried to square the idea of Mailer the fiction writer who "really couldn't finish things" with Mailer the literary figure who was "indispensable as a guide to what American letters could aim to be."

What complicates the matter is that Mailer, always intent on being not "just a writer," strove to ensure that his life (and his writing, for that matter) not be confined to the literary. He made sure his personality as well was imprinted on the culture: he married six times and had many affairs, ran for mayor of New York, publicly declared contraception to be "an abomination," jousted, sometimes physically, with cultural figures like Gore Vidal and actor Rip Torn, and, most infamously, stabbed his second wife, Adele Morales, at a party. But neither was he satisfied with being a literary celebrity. His aim, which he pursued doggedly, was to transcend the bounds of any role the world might give him.

Mailer was not the first American writer to attempt to leave a public legacy of this kind; Ernest Hemingway's global adventures were certainly a model for the man, though Mailer resented any kind of comparison. He described his reaction to *The Old Man and the Sea* in a 1952 letter to *New Yorker* writer Lillian Ross:

> I know what it is about him I can't stand. He is always saying in effect I am a man who happens incidentally to be a great writer. I know that all of you will be interested in my noble, strong, and beautiful attempts to exercise myself as a great man, and will be happy when I succeed except for professors, other writers, and assorted cocksuckers.
>
> Anyway, I thought it was good and would have been better if it hadn't been so full of shit. I thought the best thing about it was the conception of the story, but I just can't bear his prose. It sets my teeth on edge.

From the very beginning of his career, Mailer was captivated by the idea of violence and crime, and particularly by the dividing line between criminal and civilian. His approach to the topic forms a through-line from his earliest works, like his breakthrough story, "The Greatest Thing in the World," about a gambler who's beaten over a debt. You could say that all of Mailer's books take on the subject of violence in some way, with one or two exceptions, such as his biography of Marilyn Monroe.

But it was a lifelong fascination with murder in particular that may have had the greatest impact on Mailer's work and, through it, on American society at large. And it was a murder that took place a year after Mailer's birth in 1923 — so sensational it transfixed the nation and transformed the literary genre of true crime in American culture — that had the greatest influence on Mailer's ideas on murder, both in its real and literary manifestations.

In 1924, two affluent University of Chicago students named Nathan Leopold and Albert Loeb, motivated by a pseudo-Nietzschean belief in themselves as *Übermenschen*, kidnapped and murdered a 14-year-old boy named Bobby Franks. Never before had the country been confronted with a crime as heinous as the murder of a child seemingly motivated not by material gain, political ideology, poverty, or passion but by a perverse act of will. The trial that followed was billed as the "Trial of the Century" (as were two other high-profile trials of that period, one of them being the trial of Sacco and Vanzetti), and both Leopold and Loeb received life sentences.

In 1956, an author and journalist named Meyer Levin turned their story into a novel called *Compulsion*, which in April was rereleased by Fig Tree Books with a foreword by Marcia Clark, one of the prosecutors of yet another American "Trial of the Century."

By the time *Compulsion* was published, Mailer had known Levin for some years and had carried on a warm friendship with him, encouraging him and sometimes offering praise for his work (which echoed praise Levin had won for an earlier book from none other than Hemingway). Mailer would come to take something of a lifelong interest in *Compulsion* and its author, eventually listing Levin as one of four living writers deserving of the Nobel Prize — the other three were Nabokov, Henry Miller, and, of course, Norman Mailer — and, more than 30 years after the publication of the book, backing a production of it adapted for the stage by Levin.

By blending fact and fiction, Levin created what he called a "docu-novel" — a precursor to the New Journalism of the 1960s and '70s, of which Truman Capote's *In Cold Blood* and Mailer's own *The Executioner's Song* are examples — in order to explore the moral and psychological implications of a true crime. It was this innovative format that allowed Levin to offer up as serious literature a work that, on account of its lurid subject matter, might otherwise have been considered "déclassé," as fiction critic Patrick Anderson writes in his book *The Triumph of the Thriller*.

For Mailer, *Compulsion*'s marrying of a new novelistic form with sensational content constituted a "line" (as Mailer later wrote to Levin) of murder-centric American fiction that threads Theodore Dreiser's *An American Tragedy* to Mailer's own *The Executioner's Song*. *Compulsion* offered Mailer a model for using fiction to not just bring his own experience into his writing, something he'd already done in *The Naked and the Dead*, but more importantly, to smash the kinds of boundaries the writer found limiting for his own prodigious gifts.

Mailer's first real attempt at fact-infused fiction came with his fourth novel, *An American Dream* (1965), the first novel he wrote after the publication of *Compulsion*. *An American Dream* tells the story of a sexually and spiritually stymied former American congressman, talk-show host, and Harvard politics and government grad named Stephen Rojack, who one night brutally slaps his estranged wife after she tauntingly admits that she'd been unfaithful. Enraged by the affront, Rojack's wife Deborah (whose physical description closely matches that of Mailer's third wife, Jeanne Campbell) fights back by trying to knee him in the groin and then attempting — "with both hands" — to "mangle" his "root."

Rojack, a onetime war hero, strikes Deborah on the back of the neck, dropping her to one knee, and then slips her into a chokehold. Bearing down on her as he struggles against Deborah's "exceptional strength," Rojack imagines he's pushing against an enormous door "which would give inch by inch to the effort."

As Rojack continues to choke his wife, fearful that she might overpower him, an orgasm of violence

> came bursting with rage from out of me and my mind exploded in a fireworks of rockets, stars, and hurtling embers, the arm about her neck leaped against the whisper I could still feel murmuring in her throat, and *crack* I choked her harder, and *crack* I choked her again, and *crack* I gave her payment — never halt now — and *crack* the door flew open and the wire tore in her throat [...].

Disposing of his wife's body by pushing it out the window of their 10th-floor apartment, Rojack sets off on a spree of violence and sex that culminates in a confrontation with his deceased wife's incestuous, sexually abusive father, Barney Oswald Kelly (who relates that he'd invoked Satan at the moment of his daughter's conception, and ends up bestowing an accolade on our hero: "You're not bad, Stephen"). Rojack heads off to Vegas, where he fortuitously wins enough to pay off a $16,000 debt. With enough money left over for the down payment on a car, Rojack, "something like sane again," heads off on a road trip to Guatemala and Yucatán, proving the dictum that he'd laid out at the beginning of the book: "murder offers the promise of vast relief. It is never unsexual."

An American Dream was praised in a number of important reviews, including one in *National Review* by Joan Didion, who described it as a nearly "perfect novel" and "perhaps the only serious New York novel since *The Great Gatsby*." But in her classic work of feminist theory, *Sexual Politics*, Kate Millett offered a different view. Millet's devastating criticism of *An American Dream*, and its author, located the blackness at the heart of the book.

"The humanist convictions which underlie *Crime and Punishment* (the original and still the greatest study in what it is like to commit murder), may all go by the board," Millett wrote.

> Both Dostoyevsky and Dreiser, in *An American Tragedy*, gradually created in their murderers an acceptance of responsibility for the violation of life which their actions constituted, and both transcend their crimes through atonement. Rojack has some singularity in being one of the first literary characters to get away with murder; *he is surely the first hero as homicide to rejoice in his crime and never really lose his creator's support.* [Emphasis added.]

While Levin had drawn inspiration for *Compulsion* from a crime committed by others, Mailer was able to draw on his own personal experience of crime to give flesh to the fiction of *An American Dream*. Mailer wrote the book five years after what is today called the "stabbing" of Adele Morales, though with one stab wound that pierced her pericardium and a second wound to her back the attack could more accurately be described as attempted murder.

By the time of Mailer's attack on Morales, and the novel he wrote in its wake, Mailer had long been nurturing a view on violence, and in particular on murder, which had roots in his college-age ideas on traversing ethical boundaries in order to evince shock.

The overall murder rate in this country has fluctuated over the years, leaving researchers searching for a coherent theory to explain what drives its upticks and declines. Further defying the desire for a comprehensive explanation, it appears that, as American pop culture grows more accepting of depictions of violence, the murder rate has simultaneously fallen to historic lows. There has, however, been an undeniable rise in the prevalence of a certain kind of murder, that of a single (or, in the case of Columbine, double) gunman attacking civilians in public places. From Sandy Hook to Aurora to UC Santa Barbara, and the dozens of other nearly weekly crimes whose senselessness overwhelms our ability to understand them, America's feeling that mass killings are increasing is borne out by facts and statistics.

When Eric Harris and Dylan Klebold murdered 13 students at Columbine High School in 1999 the shock that rippled through the country was palpable — and lasting. Much like with Leopold and Loeb, America was shocked by not just the nature of the crimes but by the criminals themselves: Harris and Klebold, Adam Lanza, and the Aurora movie theater killer James Eagan Holmes were, unlike bogeymen of the past such as Charles Manson, Jeffrey Dahmer, Ted Bundy, or David Berkowitz, young men in their late teens or early 20s who, rather than seeking to evade capture in order to continue killing, were intent on committing a single act of appalling violence whose gruesomeness would underscore its senselessness.

Perhaps part of the shocking nature of these crimes was due to the fact that they defied not just the historical patterns of murder as they're reported in newspapers but also the traditional literary character type of the murderer, whose crime is tied to the needs of the plot and, in this sense, can be rationalized by the reader. Dostoevsky may have created the closest thing in 19th-century literature to a motiveless murderer (along with Edgar Allan Poe and the "author" of Guy de Maupassant's "Diary of a Madman"), but even Raskolnikov is driven by a need for a moral confrontation rather than an unexplained bloodlust.

While mass murders are, naturally, classified by law enforcement according to the number of victims involved, it's difficult to ignore the deeper parallels of young men like Leopold and Loeb, Harris and Klebold and Adam Lanza who, without being in a state of physical or political desperation, craft plans to hunt down innocent and unarmed victims. Most significantly, what unites them is the seemingly motiveless nature of murder committed not for money, revenge, lust, hatred, or any other discrete motivation but for the sake of the projected effect they will have on society. "The message is there is no message," James Eagan Holmes wrote in the notebook in which he also described his desire to kill and took notes on the massacre he was planning.

Connecting Mailer to this trend in murder would be like trying to show that Thackeray's *Vanity Fair* had a corrupting influence on young mothers (including those who didn't read his novel), or that Cervantes is responsible for the prevalence of delusional nostalgia among certain older men. Although the idea that art influences behavior in a direct one-to-one fashion is unsupportable (and dangerous to artistic liberty), it's difficult to deny the power of literature, and in some cases that of even a single book, to influence and shape a culture as much as it reflects the culture from which it comes.

Looking back at Mailer, who did not (by today's standards) produce an American classic comparable to *The Catcher in the Rye*, *To Kill a Mockingbird*, or *The Scarlet Letter*, it's easy to forget the outsized and almost total role he played in American culture at a defining time for this country. For more than 50 years, wherever there was a cultural moment brewing, Mailer could be found, often at its center, usually holding a lighted match. He helped define hipsterism and New Journalism, ran for office, wrote about Lee Harvey Oswald, Gary Gilmore, and Hitler, appeared in films, made films, got a convicted murderer out of jail (who killed a young man six weeks later), protested several wars, accused the CIA of murdering Marilyn Monroe, won two Pulitzer Prizes, was a punch line in a Woody Allen film and a lyric in a John Lennon song. Mailer's words had the power to draw the direct attention of sitting presidents, and his ideas formed the spearhead of a rising counterculture that thrust through the conformism of postwar America. With his celebrity status, the brilliance and originality of his thinking, and his uncanny ability to stir controversy, what Mailer did, said, and, more than anything, what he wrote mattered.

There's been no shortage of opinions on Mailer since he burst onto the literary scene with the publication of his first novel, *The Naked and the Dead*. But throughout the years, and amid all the debate, one perspective has been quietly withheld. It belongs to a nonagenarian named Harold Katz, who had the singular, if dubious, distinction of living with Mailer while the two were undergrads at Harvard in the early 1940s. Mailer had recently joined *The Harvard Advocate* and the Signet Society, the college's more intellectually oriented writer's group, and had won *Story* magazine's prize for college fiction. Katz, on the other hand, had immediately set his sights on Harvard's Zionist society, Avuka. Where Mailer was brazen, loud, and deliberately uninhibited, Katz was quiet, mannered, and devoted to his studies in politics and government.

Beyond attending parties and eating together at the Dunster House dining hall, Mailer and Katz developed a relationship that would play an important role in the development of the gifted young man who would become America's literary enfant terrible. It was a relationship that gave Katz a unique view of Mailer, making him one of the few people who not only knew both halves of the famous Mailer dyad — the bright Jewish boy from Brooklyn and the self-conscious literary entertainer — but one of the few people who witnessed the one become the other.

When it comes to the question of Mailer's legacy, Katz is (not surprisingly) of two minds. On the one hand, he sees in Mailer a brilliant and prodigious writer who could pull off both genre-bending literary feats, as he did in *The Armies of the Night*, his "non-fiction novel" on the 1967 March on the Pentagon, as well as the kind of honed and crafted storytelling Mailer was able to employ seemingly without effort. Like many of Mailer's readers, Katz, who served as an officer on a destroyer in the Pacific in World War II, can still recall the crispness — and, for him, the uncanny accuracy — of the opening scenes of *The Naked and the Dead*, Mailer's 1948 novel about a platoon of American soldiers fighting to reclaim a Pacific Island held by the Japanese.

I was introduced to Katz through a friend of his and quickly found in him far more than a repository of historical experience. He is a witty and kind man who effortlessly quotes from Dickens, and, on account of a passion for risotto, has an aficionado's acquaintance with the Tel Aviv food scene. As a writer living in Tel Aviv who grew up in suburban Southern California, virtual galaxies away from the world of mid- and late-20th-century novelists, activists, and politicians who were Katz's contemporaries and numbered among his colleagues and friends, I was drawn to the humility and charm of this erudite 94-year-old bon vivant not in spite of the six decades that separate us but in many ways because of them.

We met one winter afternoon at the city's Café Nahmani, a kind of Mideastern homage to Café de Flore, and since we'd previously discussed the puzzle of Norman Mailer, Katz handed me an article on the writer, mentioning, as he did, something about Mailer's roommate at Harvard. As I glanced over the article I asked if Katz knew who that roommate was. In response he simply said, "Me." Astonished, I asked if he'd meant to say that — some 75 years ago — he'd lived with Mailer, and he responded affirmatively.

I learned that Katz had been contacted by a number of Mailer scholars and biographers over the years, but while Mailer was alive he'd usually refused to give an interview without the writer's express consent, which was either never sought or never granted. Now, feeling there was little or no risk of harming Mailer's reputation, Katz agreed to my request for an interview.

On the topic of Norman Mailer, Katz's views are admittedly tempered by both his personal background and his college experience with the writer, though in reality, those two things are deeply intertwined. As the son of a Romanian Orthodox rabbi who immigrated to America, Katz was raised with a set of social and religious mores that were almost wholly alien to Mailer, who grew up as the precocious son of an adoring and indulgent Jewish mother and a relatively aloof, dandified father. While Katz struggled at Harvard to keep kosher as a scholarship student who couldn't afford to take his meals at a local kosher boarding house, Mailer was busily pushing the boundaries of socially acceptable behavior in virtually any way he could.

Mailer had just begun taking his first steps as a serious writer when the two were rooming together in 1941. "At this point, what became his lifestyle was now breaking out around the edges, where he was doing shocking things or saying things that were … out of the ordinary. I had no indication of his idiosyncrasies at that time, or I wouldn't have agreed to be his roommate," Katz recalls, laughing in reminiscence. "Because Norman always was — with all of his *meshugas* — he was a warm guy. And there are some aspects of him that made him sort of a loving guy. There was a sweetness about Norman when he wasn't putting on an act."

Katz had arrived in Cambridge in 1939 fresh from Terre Haute, Indiana, where he'd won a full ride to Harvard (which was awarded to him by an accountant named Alex Vonnegut, who, in addition to being president of the Harvard Club of Indiana, was also the uncle of a budding fiction writer called Kurt). After making acquaintance through Martin Lubin, the writer's freshman-year roommate, Mailer and Katz became friendly and decided to room together their junior year.

Quartered together at the country's most elite college, where, as Jews, they faced the same subtle prejudice, Mailer and Katz grew close. But despite this, and despite the common background they shared as sons of Jewish émigré parents, a peculiar dynamic evolved. Katz became for Mailer a kind of moral sounding board against which the young writer could test with increasing frequency and intensity the ethical outrageousness that would become a hallmark of his persona.

Katz remembers a typical incident involving Mailer. He was sitting in the Dunster House dining hall with Mailer and some other boys one day after getting a phone call from a Radcliffe girl who wanted to set up a date. Preoccupied with his studies, Katz had gently declined.

"You know you meet a girl casually, have a cup of coffee, take a walk with her, whatever you do, but you're not really interested, it's not going to go anywhere, you're studying, and you haven't really got time to court," Katz explains. When Mailer asked how the call had gone, Katz said he hadn't been interested. In response, Mailer spurted out: "What's the matter? *She got a wooden tit?*"

"That was, in the first place, just plain Brooklyn talk," Katz says, still showing a hint of dismay at the memory.

> We're at Harvard College, we're college boys in a very good college. And we're sitting in Dunster House dining room, where Dunster House boys sit and eat and talk about literature. […] And he thought that was an appropriate remark to make out loud in reference to some girl he'd never met.

Though the comment seems to be a clear, if minor, expression of the kind of casual misogyny for which Mailer would become notorious, in Katz's mind it was motivated not so much by an animus toward women as by a persistent and almost overwhelming need to shock. (And it's important to keep in mind that what might sound tame or even innocuous in 2015 would have sounded very different when heard in one of Harvard's dining halls in 1941. Even a full decade later, *Catcher in the Rye* would be banned for its "obscene," "blasphemous," "foul," and "filthy" language.)

According to Katz, Mailer had by that point developed a formula to produce the desired response in his Harvard classmates: "Foul language loudly stated in the midst of unsuspecting people was another way of saying, 'You guys are all uptight and I'm liberated, so let's talk about the real world and go fuck yourselves, all you.'" In Katz's view, it wasn't a set of deeply held beliefs but a need to evince shock that determined Mailer's actions, which he then distilled into ideas. But this shock calculus also shaped Mailer's understanding of his role as a writer, especially when it came to the topic of sex.

"There was a time," Katz says, still registering unease seven decades later,

> that he had gotten me and [Mailer's then-girlfriend and soon-to-be-first-wife] Bea [Silverman] into a room, saying that Bea was willing to have sex with me on the theory that they had both generously agreed that I had to be introduced to sex, and it had to be done in the right way. And, magnanimously, Bea would consent to instruct me, and Norman would not be offended. And, indeed, I suspect even now that Norman wanted to stand around and observe.

"In the first place, the whole thing is so insanely bizarre that it puts you off," Katz continues.

> You really see these people are crazy, and you don't want to deal with them. All I remember is being closeted in this suite with Norm and Bea and getting the hell out of there. It was just so insane, so crazy, so ridiculous. But that was Norman. And that was no longer a surprise.

That Mailer at age 18 believed he knew "the right way" to approach sex — that he believed there was a right way — gives pause not on account of its naïveté but because it was an attitude he carried through the rest of his life and career. Driven by the need to continually cross ethical boundaries, Mailer rigorously applied the principle of provoking outrage to the extent that what seemed like an ethical radicalism became a moralism of its own kind. At its core was an insistence on the inviolability of Manly Action and Experience, a credo that came with certain inalienable rights. For men of a certain stripe.

It was this attitude that helps explain Mailer's more outrageous outbursts, like ones he made at the now-infamous "Town Hall" debate in 1971, where a sweating and defiant Mailer took on the likes of fellow panelists Germaine Greer (whom Mailer introduced as a "formidable lady writer"), Jill Johnston, moderator Jacqueline Ceballos, who was NOW's New York chapter president at the time, and Diana Trilling. From the audience, Susan Sontag, Cynthia Ozick, Betty Friedan, and Elizabeth Hardwick quipped and challenged; at one point Ozick asked what color ink Mailer dips his testicles in. (The answer was "yellow.")

It was there that Mailer returned to the topics of violence and murder in regard to the male will, answering an audience member's question about biological determinism by saying:

> When a man is sworn that he will not strike a woman, and the woman knows that and uses it and uses it. She comes to a point where she's literally killing that man, because the amount of violence she's aroused in him, it's flooding his system and slowly killing him. So, she's engaged to that point in an act of violence and murder even though no blows are exchanged.

Far from merely an expression of his frustration with feminism, the idea behind Mailer's comment on pent-up male violence had by that time evolved into one of the underpinnings of his larger philosophy.

In 1957, a year after the publication of *Compulsion*, Mailer laid the groundwork for this idea in "The White Negro," his heralded essay on American hipsterism. In the essay, Mailer argued that if a man "cannot empty his hatred then he cannot love, his being is frozen with implacable self-hatred for his cowardice." Reaching this state of love, Mailer wrote, meant having to "replace a negative and empty fear with an outward action, even if — and here I obey the logic of the extreme psychopath — even if the fear is of himself, and the action is to murder."

Eight years after "The White Negro," Mailer published *An American Dream*, which, according to a favorable review by the eminent critic Richard Poirier, presents the "moral problem of [the book's antihero] as a murderer unpunished by law and as a sexualist who finds murder exciting […]." Mailer had already laid out much of his thinking on the idea of murder as both sexual liberation and as a pathway to love in "The White Negro," but in *An American Dream* he pushed the idea one step further by giving it a perspective and a voice.

In his review of *An American Dream*, Poirier credited Mailer — in addition only to Robert Lowell — with "having created the *style* of contemporary introspection, at once violent, educated and cool." Poirier went on to argue that looking back, people would later turn to the language of Mailer and Lowell "to determine the shapes our consciousness has been taking."

Diana Trilling took on the question of Mailer's views on violence in an essay entitled "The Moral Radicalism of Norman Mailer." In it, Trilling cited an interview Mailer had given to *Mademoiselle* (of all places) where he described a "hate-filled human" who, "grinding his boot into the face of someone, […] in the act of killing, in this terribly private moment," experiences "a moment of tenderness, for the first time perhaps in all of his existence. What has happened is that the killer is becoming a little more possible, a little bit more ready to love someone."

Trilling condemned this rationale for violence, but to her it wasn't representative so much of a moral radicalism, as her essay's title suggests, but (as Mailer himself had claimed) an antinomian return to a true morality obscured by a tradition of falsehood.

"If we listen closely," Trilling wrote,

> we perhaps hear his insistence [on violence] as less the expression of personal authority than a call to a time when religion was still a masculine discipline — a call, that is, to a Hebraic world, still molded in the image of the stern father, Moses. From Moses to

> Marion Faye [a character in Mailer's *The Deer Park*], with a stopover at Marx: Mailer's religious route is surely a strange one. But the braver efforts of culture are not always straightaway and simple.

Held on high by some of America's brightest literary lights and delivered in a style that was "violent, educated and cool," Mailer's ideas on the morality of violence trickled from the avant-garde into the mainstream of American culture. From Stephen Rojack to Travis Bickle to Patrick Bateman, a new kind of American cultural antihero began to emerge. He was a single, and explicitly white, loner who seizes control of his own fate by committing an act of senseless violence, often murder. Stuck in an absurd routine and constrained by rules he sees as arbitrary, this loner adopts the calm, calculated voice of violence to place himself at the center of an epic story of retribution. The bloodbath that ensues is a kind of perverse celebration, an unleashing of the "true self" on a society that for too long has kept it caged.

One of the many remarkable things about Mailer is that he managed to espouse an ethos of violence in a country that considers its renunciation a fundamental value. He was able to do this by skillfully manipulating his own image. When madness was called for, as when he needed to avoid a prison sentence and the moral implications of his attack on Adele Morales, Mailer was able to don that cloak. When the image of a sober, serious thinker was needed — as when he defended his lucidity and the integrity of his work in a statement after the attack, saying, "My pride is that I can explore areas of experience that other men are afraid of. I insist that I am sane" — he could simply shrug it off.

In Katz's view, Mailer's behavior was tied to career advancement. "Mailer had this cloak of insanity; he had ambitions." Katz says. It was because of this, Katz explains, that Mailer "simply didn't think any controls were justified."

Years after Harvard, Katz, then a leading Boston attorney who was fighting to advance civil rights alongside the city's progressive mayor (and the mayor's young chief of staff, Barney Frank), asked Mailer to come speak to a group of young politicians and lawyers active in Massachusetts politics. Mailer, who had just participated in the 1967 March on the Pentagon, agreed.

"He came and he spoke," Katz says.

> We had fun. But the thing about Norman was, by this time, he spoke — at least in public — in a kind of clipped English, as if he was trying to sound British and not Brooklyn. And it was a patently fraudulent accent, as if he were holding his lips and biting off his syllables. And it was sad, in a sense, because it wasn't Norman. It wasn't natural.

"When he was having a conversation with you, he would instinctively start to bob and weave as if he was a boxer," Katz says of Mailer at that time. "And he thought of himself as a macho boxer. Once he took a picture of himself with one of the boxing champions or leading fighters. He bopped one or two rounds with the guy just for the experience of boxing this world-class black boxer." Asked if he ever boxed with Mailer or saw him in the ring, Katz, who boxed throughout high school and wrestled for Harvard, says no: "He was not a boxer."

It was as if the writer of Mailer's mind had to see, to do, and to be everything to everyone. He was the Hemingway who boxed and fought in wars, the Henry Miller who scraped the mucky bottom of Paris, the Céline who chronicled the obscene futility of war, the Dos Passos who swung radically between political poles, and the T. S. Eliot who could effortlessly plumb the depths of poetry in a faux-English drawl.

But to be any of these things, Mailer had to be more than them. He had to have not just great experiences but great experiences that had not been had by those before him. He couldn't just have brilliant ideas, but he had to have the kind of brilliant ideas no one had ever dared to espouse. A call to violence for its own sake; a violence that, stripped of motive, was not just a value in its own right, but an inversion of all other values.

JOHANNA BREIDING
SHIFTS OF LAND, 2014
BLACK AND WHITE ANALOG PRINT
20 X 20"

The Man

ELIZABETH ARNOLD

I came up against it, madness.

It looked all right,
ordered even.

I went with it awhile. Then
"awhile" got
split up

hyphens everywhere glass

splintered trying to flow
instead of

stab without a will so that there

couldn't have been
wouldn't
be

ever
a thing sustained - no single

moment
holding, stretching with
the skin intact

- just the
sharp shards' glint.

The man is hardly human.

My Friend Stood Before Him

ELIZABETH ARNOLD

screaming at his face
that he was

bad, a bad man.

Drunk, leaning over him
she yelled.
                    But he just

sank a little deeper in his

leather chair, smiled,
eyes glittering

like the diamonds he'd have in his ears

had the money lasted.
To be called on

for his crimes by her

- though nothing he might
be called on for

ever could be

(by design I see now)
punishable by the state -

turned him on.

THREE WALKS ON CORN HILL BEACH

LYNNE SHARON SCHWARTZ

CORN HILL BEACH, on the bay side of Cape Cod in Massachusetts, is not far from the tip of land where the narrowing, curving peninsula of the Upper Cape yields to water. You approach Corn Hill along a path of wooden boards partially covered with sand; you look up and suddenly it's there — shore, bay, and sky — in all its understated brilliance, an oxymoron, yet it suits Corn Hill, so arresting yet so mild in character. To the north its shore sweeps a gentle arc toward Provincetown, whose notably phallic monument shows mistily in the distance, and to the south it stretches to the narrow harbor of the Pamet River, hemmed in by seaweed-strewn dunes and jagged boulders, where, bending over in the shallows, I once lost a pair of sunglasses. In the distance, nothing but sky, or the occasional Sunfish tilting in the wind. Its beauty is rivaled only by Longnook Beach on the ocean side, whose high dunes cast giant shadows as the afternoon lowers.

I chose Corn Hill as the best place to walk away the hours of my brother's ordeal by surgeon's knife till the phone call would come to relieve my mind, or not. Beyond its splendor, it is historically significant, not only publicly but privately. A plaque proclaims it to be the spot where the Pilgrims first landed, although several other plaques on the Cape claim this distinction as well, so the Pilgrims seem to have made several stops. Its private history goes back over 40 years, to the summers we first came here with our small children and they found beach friends, instant intimacies that sprang up during the construction of forts and moats or hunting for hermit crabs to place in buckets of water where they flailed about, and ended abruptly when the parents were ready to go home.

I walked past the scattered blankets and umbrellas, today's children building their castles and moats in the mud. It was morning; there weren't yet many people about. I walked in the direction of the harbor and was soon alone, not far from the section set aside by the thinnest of cords, almost invisible, for the nesting terns, which with a touch of arrogance would spread their great wings to glide over the bay. Not like the plebeian seagulls who wandered about picking at crumbs and bits of shells smelling of fish. Or the much smaller sandpipers who appeared in late afternoon hopping about like marionette birds controlled by strings.

I was trying to tire myself out until I was too tired to worry about my brother, so I walked all the way to the harbor, where I stood on the rocks and watched a few small boats pull in and be hoisted up to shore on a broad slanted gangplank. On the way back I stopped and sat on the sand. I had a sudden urge to swim. The water looked so inviting; it drew me powerfully. But I had no bathing suit; I hadn't planned to swim, only walk. I must have thought that bringing a bathing suit would denote a pleasure trip, while I was dedicating the hours to worrying. It seemed wrong, somehow, to set out for a swim while my brother was having his chest broken open. I was even faintly guilty about being away on vacation while he was lying on that table, but there was no help for that — he'd been stricken suddenly.

I wanted very badly to swim. I looked around; no one was in sight. I hesitated to take off my clothes and plunge in. I dithered for a few moments till at last I thought, the hell with it, my brother is having his bare chest invaded, surely I can find the courage to take off my clothes. I stripped off my shorts and shirt and went in the water in nothing but bra and underpants. I felt very daring. I splashed around, swam a bit, floated on my back, and watched the lazy clouds bump into each other. I was quite pleased at having done exactly what I wanted, casting aside inhibition.

I didn't rush out, and when I finally went ashore I didn't hurry to put on my clothes. I had to walk all the way back with my wet underwear under my shorts and shirt but this did not spoil my pleasure. If my brother had not survived I might have felt guilty but as it turned out he did survive.

Several years later, I went again to Corn Hill to minister to my grief, a different kind of grief this time. (My brother was fine now, hale as before, and often when I phoned he answered panting because he was running on the treadmill in his basement.) This time I didn't walk. I sat on the beach on a towel, staring at the water but seeing the images I'd seen on television the night before in a bar, since my apartment had no TV. A friend I'd made in town and I had tickets to a play at the Provincetown Inn, a play about the relationship between Eleanor Roosevelt and her journalist friend and probable lover, Lorena Hickok. We didn't know what else to do with ourselves given the morning's attacks in New York under a dazzlingly blue sky, so we went to see the play, though we felt slightly uncomfortable, even oddly disloyal, doing so. The play was distracting, but as soon as it was over our thoughts returned to the events in New York, and we went into a bar to see the images again.

As I sat on my towel staring at the images in my head, a man and a woman walked by in their bathing suits. The woman was crying; her hands covered her face. The man had his arm around her shoulders. I understood her and felt just as she did, though I wasn't crying aloud and I didn't feel like walking, only sitting. And I was up here alone, not on a family vacation but working. I was staying in a small apartment in Provincetown for the month of September and would drive to the beach when I judged I had done enough work for the day. Today I hadn't done any work at all, just made some phone calls, or tried to. The lines were mostly tied up. The automated voice kept saying try your call later.

It was afternoon now, high tide. The tides shift back and forth roughly every six hours. In other years, when I was here with my family, some days we'd stay at the beach long enough to watch the tide go out and see the sunset; or we'd return to Corn Hill at low tide to watch the sun sink into the bay like a huge cookie dipped very slowly into frosting. A crowd would gather in the evening as at a performance. The sun going down, however spectacular, was nothing strange, but the change in the bay was very strange indeed, though we had seen it happen many times. Where there had been water deep enough to swim in, there were mud flats, dotted with shells and small rocks, interspersed with shallow puddles. The setting sun glinted on the thin patina of water covering the mud, making it glow orange and gold. We could walk far out on the flats, maybe close to a quarter of a mile, much farther than we would have swum at high tide. Despite the tides' schedule of every six hours, more or less, for reasons I can't explain it was often at its lowest in the evening when the sun was setting.

There were people swimming that afternoon, though not as many as usual. Children clambered around on plastic tubes and giant plastic animals, and others carried pails of sand back and forth from their building sites. But a curious hush hung over the beach, as if even the children were softening their shouts out of respect for the thousands of dead, and there were fewer encampments of blankets and umbrellas than usual, or fancy big tents in vivid colors, as if they hesitated to disrupt the general sobriety by their dazzle.

After a while I made myself get up and drive to the main pier in Provincetown to meet the ferry from Boston. My daughter would be on it. She was coming up to meet me and share the drive home to New York, because in my mood of shock and desolation I couldn't face the six-hour drive by myself. I parked and walked way out on the pier to where the boats docked. Many people were gathered, as always, to meet the ferry. They were in bright shirts and shorts and colorful sleeveless dresses and they were tanned. We could see the ferry when it was still far out in the bay; then it rounded the breakwater and approached. It lumbered in, the gangplanks were lowered, and the passengers appeared, dragging their suitcases on wheels. I had seen this scene many times. People greeted their friends and relatives on the pier, falling into each other's arms. A few looked as stunned as I felt, as the woman on the beach had been, but most of them greeted each other gaily, as always when the ferry docked. I didn't look at them very closely though; I was watching for my daughter. Finally she appeared, not dragging a suitcase but wearing a backpack. She would stay only a night or two and then we would go home.

Even from a distance her face looked as if it had been dipped in ashes. I studied some of the others from the ferry more closely and their faces had the same ashy look. My daughter gazed around at the scene — all the lively features of a summer resort — as if she had disembarked onto another planet. She said that after the hours in New York following the attack, the scene struck her as surreal — the people dressed like tropical birds, hugging and slapping each other's backs and hurrying off to their cars to begin a long beach weekend. She didn't want to talk much. We got in the car and drove to the apartment I was renting but would be leaving very soon. All I wanted was to be at home, closer to the rubble.

On another afternoon as I walked along the edge of the shore at Corn Hill (no shock or anxiety this time, just a pleasant beach day), I came upon a woman with a digital camera taking photos, or maybe a video, of her husband — I assumed it was her husband — and their three young children frolicking in the water. The woman was pretty far up on the sand and the man and children maybe a dozen feet off in the water, so to avoid being in the photo I would have had to diverge from my path and walk a broad arc around her. I didn't feel like doing that. I didn't know the etiquette for digital cameras — this was when they were new. Naturally if the photographer and her object had been only a few feet apart I would have walked politely around her; also, it struck me as odd to take a photo from so far off. So I walked in the path of the photography.

Somewhere, someday, when the woman shows her photos or video, a viewer will ask, Who's that?, meaning the woman in the black-and-white bathing suit going by. Oh, just someone passing on the beach, she'll say, and that will be all.

I will exist, or rather my image will exist, in their photo archives. That couple was much younger than I. In their archives my image, proof of my existence, will outlast me. Just a stranger passing by, with no history or identity beyond what can be seen from a distance in an amateur photo: a middle-aged woman, on the small side, dark curly hair, in a black-and-white one-piece bathing suit. A person who once existed and passed through their lives with no impact whatsoever (unless you count the interruption), and of no significance whatsoever. When I recall that moment or imagine that family, years from now, looking over old vacation photographs, I have a fleeting urge to let them know that I am — or was — something more than a stranger passing through their sight line, someone with a complete identity, whose life did have an impact on and significance for many others. Someone who had walked on that beach many times, usually reveling in its beauty, but on occasion dazed and grief-stricken. But of course that would be impossible, and moreover it's not a very strong urge. More of a mild notion, the way you don't especially care what will happen after you're dead, in regard to many things you care passionately about now.

JOHANNA BREIDING
SWINGS, 2014
BLACK AND WHITE ANALOG PRINT
20 x 20"

Rush BARRIE JEAN BORICH

THE LED BUS STOP SIGN says the next arrives in 13 minutes, but damn I'm due in 10, glancing back in case the bus creeps up from behind, going, going, getting there just one minute late, but cramped, panting. My vow: (to whom?) NEXT TIME I leave early, I stroll, like the businessmen I observed when visiting Italy, ambling across piazzas, leather folios tucked under arms, no hurry, living their commute.

For decades I've had this rushing trouble, so bad the year I'm 17 my friend with a car picks me up for school, a rescue from my daily six-block pummel through yards, between garbage receptacles, through shrubbery, and damn damn damn another slow-moving freight blocks my crossing into the school grounds again. I eye the spaces between boxcars. Can I pull myself over the coupling without getting hurt? I don't try, but the image hiccups as I pant, rush-waiting until I can resume the forward charge.

In middle age the lure of comfort makes me late, the luxury of this (not the next) suspended moment. I don't dress because my chair is pleasing. I can't rush my coffee — an Americano, or *lungo* to be specific (even the name is slow), from the espresso machine we bought after a lingering trip across Italy. Experts speak of delayed gratification, say I'm wrong to want what I want when I want, but I'm suspicious of such regulation. The hell with YOU dead-old pleasure-haters.

And yet, I sweat, drop gloves, bruise shins pushing through train turnstiles (oh that explains the mystery bruise). And what of when I'm too old to run, or the knee I wrench on the L steps won't heal? Who must I make myself over to be to walk to work the Italian way? I contemplate over another lungo until I'm late again, and so I mentally reorganize, cancel the dawdling coffee I'd planned for later, along the way, if I'm not rushing.

A Thief in the Night

ISHION HUTCHINSON

Rain is falling throughout; occasional soft and hard thunders.

Something making noise tonight again.
Is who there, eh? Boy, my child, you there,
you sleeping? O God, guard you! Something
wicked out there. I hear it long, from I
dreaming I hear it stirring. But crosses,
what a thing to come here tonight?
Boy, boy? Christ, you there, wake up!

Mama! Mama!

What happen, what wrong?

You never hear him,

you not hear him disturbing the basil?

No, Mama. Hear what? Nothing wrong, you
dreaming again because Pa gone, is because him gone.

No! No! Lord, my God, no. I hear it like how
a thief enter. Thief, O God, is a thief,
and him in here boy; shhh. Come.

Mama?

Don't talk, son, is so the vampire strike;
him smell your breath first and then him smell
your young blood and then him know your heart
beat and then him can find you in the dark.

But Mama,

I hear nothing – nothing. I going check.

No!
Boy, him out there, ready to blood you. Stay here,
we wait. O God of Salvation, protect us
from evil till Thine Kingdom come! You hear
him there, a torment us? Hear him?

Hear what, Mama?
Please, Mama, there is nothing there and you
making mi frighten.

Child, you not hear him?
The spirit-thief?
I hear nothing.

Him talking!

I come here tonight, black as sin ownself,
drunk nuh rass, like when two mongrels latch
up together, and I come conjoined as two thing,
and I come, like I say, for I is man of importance,
as spirit-thief, that thief, mind you, don't creep
through poor people window, like them two
there so, and then jump fence with they poultry,
I don't fold that way though I play foul to catch
wise; I come to this tomb-space hovel for I have
importance of the spirit. So important that
tonight, that bloodclaat moon, full drunk,
give me light to thief one of them tonight,
and since my Master like them fresh like calf
in the mourning, excuse me tongue, I mean
morning of their lives, you must know who I want.
Not that old fowl. I going suck him dry, drier
than the fool, is Pa, I sucked dry to hell!

Guard me spirit, the vile thing right here
with we now.

Mama. Mama, what? Nothing not –

The thief, boy, the thief.

Yes, the thief. Is me. But I really do
prefer ambassador. Ambassador Thief.

Mama, there's no –

Him right here so, stink of sulphur.

The old higue
got a good nose. Yes, I am yellow-hearted,
combustible, I am leaves ready to catch fire
and burn this little one with me down to Avernus!

No, no, not him! You can't take him, take me!
Do, take me!

Woman, hush it, for what seal
with the wax tongue of my boss cannot open.
That mean it well embossed, you see me?
Your man feel him was Christ in senility,
sacrificing himself for you and the little kid.
Right now him a bleat under the scorch a hell,
to rass! My Don, Hot Man of the Underworld,
forking him up now, and your man farting up.
So I just come to redress this small heist,
for right now Bossy vex vex that I never take
the sapling down to him, instead I take pity
and hear out the grandfather, took him instead.
But the Big Man wrath on me: "My orders is law.
When I say bring a thing I just mean that thing."
The Man get all brighter than the morning sun,
and you know, is for the sun him name?
Yes, real star, lucem ferre, so I just come to collect.

Almighty Father! No, back away out this house.
You not getting him.

                              Mama, mama? What you
talking, who you talking to? who want me?
No Mama, stop now, I here, holding you
and there is nothing here; me and you one.
Mama, I sorry too that him gone, but you
said dead is dead and dead is gone.

But the little chick philosophic, man,
balance in the flesh, and I can't wait
to weigh it on my teeth. So succulent.

No, you vampire, take me, take me,
take me, take me, take me, take me.
You come here before, hungry for flesh,
and my man, my husband who work out
him soul case on him farm and in the church,
give himself to you. Me pray till blood come
a me eyes, me band me belly, and pray,
pray until the Holy Spirit say no more,
no more will the thiefing devil enter me house.
But look now, again, me old tired self,
me who so near the grave hole, no husband,
because the man know when you come here
the first time, him know, for him give up himself
so you could spare the boy, and spare me
just a little while longer, just to stay here
and see to it him get little bigger for the world.
And who fault that? Devil in hell! And see
you come back tonight, and you hungry
for soft flesh, hungry for my grandson.
But crosses, man, what me ever do people?
All me born days me show love and peace,
greet them at daylight, "Mornin' to you"
and if night ever catch me on the road,
"G'dnight to you." And from me know
myself, only one man ever know me,

and him dead and gone, this one man here …
Hus … hel … band … help, the devil is in your house,
husband, in your house you build with your two
hands. Darling, my man, come back to your house.
Come take charge. Is you make it, your sweat
and blood, not this backside devil! Husband!
Oh Lord, husband, your poor woman alone
with the little boy can't fight him. Come back.
Wherever you there now, come back. Is me
calling you, come back, is me, me your wife.
I call you back, come back.

                                        Stop the preaching,
it not Sunday, and all this tongue-lashing
can't bring back what already digest. Burp.
Now, on to the task at hand, the boy: come.

How you shaking so, Mama? Why the lamp
jumping so and why it so cold now, Mama?

Is the devil.

                    Is me.

                                        I numb.

                                                        Boy?

ALEX OLSON
COCO, 2009
OIL ON CANVAS
41 X 29"
COURTESY OF LAURA BARTLETT GALLERY, LONDON

UNNATURAL DISASTERS, OR QUEERING KATRINA

JONATHAN ALEXANDER
PHOTOS BY JON HUGHES / PHOTOPRESSE

LATE MARCH in New Orleans, a bit humid, but not unbearably so for just past midday. I'm about to board a van with a bunch of strangers who have all signed up for a Katrina tour, a three-hour survey of the devastating floods that submerged 90 percent of the city in the aftermath of the hurricane and the failure of the levee system. Folks from New Jersey, Illinois, and even Canada talk excitedly about water damage and urban blight. Almost 10 years to the day and the floods still fascinate.

Besides our guide, I'm the only one from New Orleans. I was born and raised here, but I'm not telling anyone. I'm undercover, a closeted native. I want to experience the tour as a visitor, a stranger, as someone whose family wasn't impacted by Katrina and the flooding. I want some distance. Or maybe I want to erase the distance I have felt from this place; to remember, to reflect, to live all of it again. Approaching the 10-year anniversary of the event, which memories are important? I left New Orleans over 20 years ago; a queer man struggling with his sexuality in the Deep South, I needed to leave to find myself in less hostile places. I'm torn. This has been home and not home. I wonder — after time, the storm, the flooding, the blood in the water — what it can be to me now.

The tour is one of many you can get in and around NOLA, with visits to the French Quarter and old plantations just upriver being some of the most popular. I am surprised that Katrina tours are still so in demand. I had to call around to a couple of places before finding an empty seat in a van that accommodates about 12. I get to ride shotgun with the tour guide, a guysy guy in a Saints ball cap, a native New Orleanian, someone I could've gone to high school with in Metairie, the large suburb to the west, just over the 17th Street Canal. He's been a guide for well over a decade and knows his stuff, winding the van through the old city's small streets, up Canal, around the French Quarter (streets closed for one of the many outdoor music fests), and into the Faubourg Marigny, one of the oldest neighborhoods near downtown. He jokes throughout the tour and is particularly playful with the kids on the van, testing their knowledge of historical events. But a certain seriousness lurks in the background. Constant reminders of flood levels, references to famous buildings that no longer exist, details of renovations undertaken since the waters receded. We can't go into the lower Ninth Ward apparently. According to our guide, city officials have put the area on a "no tour"

list. Some of the wood used in the Brad Pitt homes (Pitt's Make It Right organization built over a hundred sustainable homes in the area) is apparently rotting, not having been treated to withstand the abundant moisture in the area. (Pitt's foundation is suing the supplier.)

While most of the afternoon focuses on Katrina, our guide weaves in some other local color, particularly the famous above-ground tombs. When your city is largely six-plus feet below sea level, you don't bury people in the ground. We pull over to walk around an old cemetery, dates in the family vaults stretching way back into the 19th century. As new generations pass, old remains are swept to the back and fall to the bottom, piling on top of one another over the years.

Thinking of the dust of generations easily recalls scenes from almost exactly a decade ago. My sister called on a Sunday, sobbing into the phone, just days after the storm and reports of the flooding were being televised nonstop. My dad wouldn't live much longer. He'd been suffering from Parkinson's for well over a decade, his health slowly deteriorating. The last year had been particularly rough, the physical and cognitive debilitation having taken a sharp turn for the worse. I had visited earlier in the summer, at my mother's insistence, to give her a hand. As his primary caretaker and approaching 70 herself, she was wearing out. It wasn't a pretty sight. In the middle of the night I found him stark naked and standing over his bathroom sink, water running, his body rigid and paralyzed. The water had woken me up. He had no idea what was happening or how he'd gotten there, but I was able to get him back into bed.

That was about a month before Katrina. I had no reason to doubt my sister's assessment of the situation or the deep pain in her voice when she told me I should come as soon as I could. Kissing my partner, Mack, goodbye, I was on a plane the next day.

Getting into the area wasn't going to be easy. New Orleans International Airport was completely shut down except for emergency and military traffic. Same for roads in and out of the city. My parents had retired to the Mississippi Gulf Coast, to a spot pretty much in the direct path of Katrina. In the dead of night, having stayed up to watch incoming reports about the storm's predicted trajectory, they'd been able to get across New Orleans and make it all the way to west Louisiana, outside of Lake Charles, near the Texas border, where much of my mother's extended family still live. She's from tough Cajun stock, the French country people who, expelled from Canada once the British took over, settled in the swamps and watery byways of southwest Louisiana. It's remote country, inhospitable, hot and humid. Of the numerous small towns between Baton Rouge and Houston, Lake Charles is among the largest. After a flight from Cincinnati to Houston, and a puddle jumper into Lake Charles, my brother-in-law picked me up at the airport.

My mother and I slept in the waiting room that night, fitfully, having pulled together a few uncomfortable vinyl-covered chairs, surrounded by other evacuees waiting out news of their loved ones. In the morning, my mother, sister, and I stood around my father's bed, holding vigil over his pitifully wasted form, his breaths coming in slow but jagged. His face pinched in unconsciousness, he wouldn't ever open his eyes again. The nurses assured us it was only a matter of time.

My father died about 10 hours after I arrived. His frail body and mind couldn't handle the stress of the evacuation. My mother was convinced the overtaxed hospital staff couldn't attend to him properly. He was a Katrina victim, one of many old, sick people who didn't survive the storm. He was fortunate to die in a bed, with family surrounding him.

Days later, we had his funeral and then waited for permission to get back into the affected areas to see what remained. For weeks, many folks were stuck in west Louisiana. My mother, sister, and brother-in-law, along with their three kids, stayed with an aunt and her adult children, many of whom lived in trailers or homes they'd built around their mother's trailer, off a small road that bore their family name. The water would often run brown for a bit when you turned on the tap. Eventually we learned that my sister's and mother's homes had negligible damage. An aunt, uncle, and their sons, though, had lost everything, flooded out of the city.

The people in the tour van want to see blight. There's not as much of it as there used to be. In 2006, I drove to the area with a photojournalist, Jon Hughes, to do a story about the devastation. The storm surge had taken out nearly every building along Highway 90, the beachfront road on the Mississippi Gulf Coast. We saw miles and miles of abandoned homes that had sat under 9 to 12 feet of water. Plenty of blight.

Nine years later, driving through the upper Ninth Ward, we see a destroyed home here and there, desolate with orange spray-painted X's still noting when the building had been inspected for remains, human and otherwise. Mostly we see newer homes now elevated, as much as 10 feet off the ground, with carports holding empty the space for future floodwaters. Our guide points out how older homes had been lifted up, or just moved completely to somewhat higher ground. He talks about his home in Lakeview, flooded under eight feet of water, and the weeks and weeks of driving into the neighborhood with family to salvage, clean up, repair, and rebuild, returning to Baton Rouge after dark when the curfew came.

Habitat for Humanity and the city built the 72 homes of Musicians' Village, centered on the Ellis Marsalis Center for Music, providing music instruction for area youth. Brightly colored in oranges, purples, greens, a creole medley, they house local players, an attempt to preserve the city's jazz heritage.

The wrecked and abandoned, next to the colorfully new, hopeful for the future.

I was a strange child, gangly and cross-eyed, hardly athletic, bookish, marked as a faggot long before I had consciousness of my own sexual impulses or proclivities. I was fortunately tall for my age so suffered little physical abuse, but the taunts were constant and corrosive. Even some teachers at the various Catholic schools we attended identified me as the class queer. In one awful incident during my freshman year (burned in my brain), the health teacher was recounting stories of a buddy who worked in an emergency room. Worst of all, he said, far worse than the car wrecks, the fistfights, the violence, were the faggots who had stuck things up their asses and couldn't get them out. Disgusting. The teacher's buddy had once put a probe up some poor queer's butt only to find a light staring back, a flashlight in the guy's ass. The class screamed in raucous, titillated disgust while I, vaguely aware that they were talking about someone like me and everybody knew it, could only squirm in my seat, already ashamed.

My mother did what she could to encourage and help me defend myself, but my father could not. He was the first relative to ask me if I was queer. He'd probably always wondered, and he let me know he was repulsed. I learned later that he suspected I wasn't actually his child — a feat of real denial: from the shape of my face, not to mention my thinly fine hair, anyone can see I am an Alexander.

When I was younger, even as a teenager, I dreamed about leaving. I knew I didn't belong. I retreated into books and church. Fantasy and science fiction transported me to other realms of possibility, while thrice-weekly church services (Sunday morning and evening, plus Wednesday night prayer meetings) fortified me to turn the other cheek, to forgive those who hurt me, to trust that I too would one day inherit the earth. I hoped for just a little piece of it that would feel safe.

When folks learn I'm from Louisiana, they often remark first on my relative lack of accent, and then about how wonderful it must have been to grow up in such a fascinating place. Bourbon Street, Mardi Gras, letting the good times roll. But my experience of New Orleans involved little revelry. As in many old European-esque cities with carnival traditions, periods of excess are strictly contained, kept within strict spaces and times. Sure, as a young man, I could head to the French Quarter and drink myself into stupidity about the boy who wasn't going to love me back, but then I'd have to return to the suburbs of flesh-denying self-hatred. I escaped in my mid-20s before slitting my wrists in a bathtub.

In a beautiful poem about the city, "before the storm: geographers in new orleans," Romanian-born American poet Andrei Codrescu writes about how his adopted city instills in its inhabitants a "knowledge of finitude that is intimately woven into our psyches / and that urges us to live intensely before the assured cataclysm." Growing up, we always felt the "assured cataclysm," quite physically. Nearly every hurricane season we'd be packing the car to head west or north, fleeing a storm. We always knew that the city would eventually flood. The protecting levees were destined to fail. The waters that receded would surely rise again. New Orleans knows the cycles of life, celebrates them in its many festivals and its contradictions: its intense love of pleasure and its tolerance of corruption, its nurturing of the bon vivant and its deep racial segregations, its sexual openness and its intense homophobia.

The schools and churches that gave me a love of reading and music also taught me to hate myself. The relatives who fed me their delicious food withheld their love. Even after the storm, as we huddled in my aunt's trailer outside Lake Charles, my father just passed, my mother and sister wondering if their homes still existed, one relative offered that Katrina was God's punishment on New Orleans for its sinful ways, and another complained to my aunt that Mack, my partner of 15 years, who had made it into the area for my father's funeral, shouldn't be allowed to stay in her trailer. We ate our boudin and shrimp creole, and I could only thank the god who had struck my hometown that I'd escaped, however scarred.

One of New Orleans's nicknames is "the city that care forgot." I felt I knew those forgotten cares well. I can sometimes still feel them, ghost bruises.

But in our tour guide's tone I hear a care that I'd not noticed before, or perhaps one that I didn't know how to hear. Maybe it's one that only Katrina and the failure of the levees could make audible for me. We stop at the 17th Street Canal, site of the most devastating levee breach of all. The guide's voice strains a bit. He's been talking for nearly three straight hours, but I sense something else

happening. He's getting riled. He points out the massive construction — new walls, new pumps, new floodgates — but he's not proud. He wonders why all this wasn't here before. The van slows down so we can see the historical plaque marking the location of the breach. It's a typical brown piece of metal, and the guide reads the words with increasing emphasis, his voice cracking at the end:

> On August 29, 2005, a federal floodwall atop a levee on the 17th Street Canal, the largest and most important drainage canal for the city, gave way here causing flooding that killed hundreds. This breach was one of 50 ruptures in the federal Flood Protection System that occurred that day. In 2008, the US District Court placed responsibility for this floodwall's collapse squarely on the US Army Corps of Engineers; however, the agency is protected from financial liability in the Flood Control Act of 1928.

An "ooh" escapes from the back of the van, but we are otherwise silent until someone points to some of the houses around the levee, asking why anyone would want to live here again. The guide almost loses composure. Sitting in the front with him, I see his hands clench and unclench, the healthy pink of his face reddening a bit more. "This is the important part. We didn't ask to be flooded. Blame Uncle Sam."

I have to admit, I like his anger. I'm glad he's pissed. He should be. And he shouldn't tolerate the questioning from the back of the van, wondering why and what someone would *choose*: this is his home.

I am trying to understand how Katrina changed things for me. It's complicated. The storm, my father's death — a welter of ambivalent feelings and memories of my boyhood. Perhaps

abandonment is a key here. I had abandoned New Orleans, feeling it had abandoned me, just as I had been emotionally abandoned by my father, and by a social world and Catholic doctrine that bullied and degraded me. I had decided to leave this place, that had left me first, and parent myself in another state.

In the aftermath of the storm, as I sat with my family, flooded out, my particular relationship to New Orleans was exposed, requiring an accounting of the bodies I'd left behind. And how could I think of those bodies, those intimacies bloating in my mind, and not think too on my own queerness, the queerness that drove me from my home?

As I held my father in my arms while he died, I realized his lack of affection hadn't completely damaged my own ability to love. Finally, nearly two weeks after the storm, my father's ashes packed in the car, we were able to get across the city back to our family houses — my mother's outside of Bay St. Louis in Mississippi, directly in the path of the storm, my sister's in Mandeville on the north shore of Lake Pontchartrain. Some shingles missing, some food wasted. Otherwise everything was all right.

I rode back with my cousin, just a couple of years older than me, someone I hadn't seen in two decades, possibly more. A devout man, he was generous of spirit, unlike many Christians I've known. He told me that he and his siblings had often wondered about me. I braced myself, but then he clarified. They'd wondered, but not because I'd been cast out: I was the one who had gotten away. They were intrigued, curious. They'd often imagined what it would be like to leave, though few of them ever did. I'd never even imagined such a perspective: that others, my cousins, could envy, even in a small way, my having moved on. That they identified in me a courage I couldn't acknowledge myself; I'd felt it, not as courage, but as the only way to survive.

A small thing? Maybe. But Katrina enabled me to hear it.

There is part of me that thinks of Katrina all the time.

Part of my fascination is its avoidability. Surely a Category 5 hurricane is a force to be reckoned with. But the damages exacerbated by human failing, by human negligence, demand an accounting. So do the damages done to me, a young queer man, drowning in waves of homophobia.

There are many Katrina stories. Jed Horne's *Breach of Faith: Hurricane Katrina and the Near Death of a Great American City* offers a compelling overview of the personal and political dimensions of the catastrophe. Sheri Fink chronicles the experiences of medical staff and patients trapped in a hospital in her *Five Days at Memorial*, based on her Pulitzer Prize–winning journalism. In the form of a graphic novel by Josh Neufeld, *A.D.: New Orleans After the Deluge* presents multiple stories of folks surviving the flooding and trying to rebuild their lives. Others had it worse. If Spike Lee's *When the Levees Broke* makes anything clear to me, it's the extent to which our family was lucky. My immediate family, at least. We lost my father, but that loss in itself seemed a relief, given how long he'd been ill. We were with him when he died, in a hospital, not belly down in some toxic sludge of floodwater, left for dead days after the storm came and went, the waters rose and fell. We were luckier than we knew at the time.

I still feel lucky, sitting in this van, touring the damage, having survived.

Katrina has affected my feelings about New Orleans. I have started to fall a little bit in love with NOLA and the Gulf Coast. I remember one day, months after the storm, walking along the beach in Bay St. Louis, surveying the sustained damage. Someone had set up a Christmas tree on the beach amidst the debris. Hope in the middle of destruction.

I want to hope, but mine is a cautious love, for sure. Love is risky, isn't it? Perhaps there's nothing more here for me than the beginnings of a change of heart. A strange sense of protectiveness about the place I had stopped calling home. A strange desire to call it home again, or perhaps for the very first time.

JOHANNA BREIDING
TWO SANDBAGS, 2014
BLACK AND WHITE ANALOG PRINT
20 X 20"

Visiting Prophets

HAFIZAH GETER

1

My uncle pacing the dirt field behind his mother's house,
like a car whose tank will not empty.
He might as well be in prison.

Poisoned

We guess,

bipolar

2

that maybe the malaria
is at it again.

If this were America, he would be a boat we could tug
beneath the shed during winters,

could thaw him
without having to send word
to other seasons. Not even money would stop
us from feeding him medicated morsels
to bring his mind back in from the rain.

At the very least we could fix this fucking
limp.

If this were anywhere, we would be hysterical.
So long it's been since relief has doubled

us over, cried into our stomachs,
held our knees to our shoulders.

3

But since this is our homeland, we drive.

Through markets.
Past Ahmadu Bello University,
where my father taught students to draw the body
after mastering the line.

4

Into the brunt of a fresh
rainy season, my cousin snakes
the car round the roundabout,
round beggars using foreign objects
as limbs. We are stockpiling

mangos, plantains, a bit
more powdered milk,
and baobab leaves for kuka.

Guards barely old enough to be lovers
stand in front of gated compounds
avoiding eyes and forgetting
the weight of their weapons, forgetting
our mothers have died
the same way.

5

What do we name this revision
of our bodies?

Diabetes
Hypertension
Hepatitis
Stroke

I can see how all these guns have helped
keep my uncle crazy.

Our hunger is anonymous.

6

For three days my feet continue
to swell, splitting

the stitching of the boots that took my last
eighty dollars. Not even
Nikes can hold me.

Maybe, my uncle
is onto something,

pacing the backyard for his madness.

7

On our mothers' dirt
roads we know

how dangerous someone who wants to save you
can become.

Compassion is not the same as repair.

8

Let's say madness has a heart. ⫽

HOW A WILD PIG MAY UPROOT THE TREE OF LIFE

GREG CRITSER

Who knows of every tryst in the depths of the wood? Who can number the illegitimate pleasures shared by creatures of separate species?

— Buffon, 1770

IN 1994, paleontologist Stephen Jay Gould — arguably the most celebrated postwar thinker in his field — attended a conference on evolution. It was a familiar arena for Gould. Since the early 1970s, he'd been articulating and, alternately, defending his seminal work on what he termed "punctuated equilibrium." Gould had succeeded in convincing many scientists, especially other paleontologists, that the fossil record simply did not support the scientific consensus about evolution — the belief that the process by which a new type of organism typically arises is a slow accumulation of minor changes over time. The fossils don't show that, Gould said, because there are no "transitional forms." That is, from looking at fossils, it seems that organisms come into being abruptly, via "punctuation." And thereafter, the typical fossil organism does not gradually change, he said, it simply exists in the same form until it becomes extinct. He dubbed this lack of change "equilibrium" or "stasis."

Many of his fellows saw this as a kind of scientific creationism. The mere use of the term "transitional forms" was a red flag in conversations about evolution and creationism.

Punctuated equilibrium troubled many biologists because it neutered natural selection. If the typical fossil form changed in no way whatsoever, it certainly wasn't going to change under the influence of natural selection.

But punctuated equilibrium was an observation about fossils *over time*. Gould said little about how such a process might actually work. It is a question that has stuck in the craw of establishment scholars; try as they might, they have yet to entirely reckon his work — his observed fact — with their own ideas of how evolution occurs.

The situation might be called intellectual stasis.

Still, rogue ideas sometimes break through. During coffee at that 1994 conference, Gould bumped into a tousle-haired genetics graduate student named Eugene McCarthy. McCarthy told Gould he agreed with his basic observations, but he wanted to talk about mechanisms that might account for them. "I remember asking him, you know, well, how does it work, what is the mechanism?" McCarthy says. "He looked at me and said, 'I don't know. I am just presenting a known fact, *an observed fact*. Someone else will have to find out how it works.'"

McCarthy had long pondered a hypothetical answer to that question, what he called "stabilization processes." Under that heading he lumped a variety of well-known genetic mechanisms (many of which involve hybridization) that rapidly produce new stable forms of life. For example, polyploidization, a process that creates offspring that have one or more extra sets of chromosomes than their parents do. The change takes a single generation and can alter many traits that remain stable in subsequent generations. As McCarthy saw it, such mechanisms could account for Gould's punctuation and stasis.

In the theory McCarthy constructed on the basis of these processes, "natural selection" is not the same thing that Darwin described. In the traditional view of evolution, there is competition among individuals in which those who leave more offspring pass on more of their genes, and thus prevail. In McCarthy's world, natural selection involves competition not between individuals but between "forms." In other words, some stable forms of life persist longer than others and give rise to more offspring forms. As a result, their traits spread to more progeny forms than do those forms of life that have fewer offspring.

This formulation of natural selection in terms of forms means that different forms of life can be successful in different ways, because under stabilization theory it makes no difference whether *individuals* compete or cooperate. You can have successful forms in which individuals compete, like sharks, or you can have successful forms in which individuals cooperate, like bees. Thus, where mainstream biologists see evolution as "red in tooth and claw," McCarthy sees it as a process where unselfishness and cooperation can often make evolutionary sense. Things mate that shouldn't mate. Forms thrive until they're spent, and then they're *gone*. McCarthy's is an ancient realm of free love, partying in happy stasis until the extinction police arrive.

McCarthy is an expert on bird hybrids, having written an exhaustive reference work on the subject for Oxford University Press. He has been working for years on a similar book about mammalian hybrids and has investigated the possible hybrid origins of human beings. He has even proposed exactly what kind of beastly lovers might long ago have mated to produce *Homo sapiens*: a primate resembling a bonobo and an ancestor of the ordinary pig.

As one might expect, discussing McCarthy's pig-primate hypothesis in the scrum of modern media can be awkward. In the summer of 2013, when reporters first discovered his website and began writing about the idea, some rated him as irresponsible, uninformed, naive, and even just this side of mad. Jimmy Kimmel had his predictable fun with it all — a mocked-up video clip of a McCarthy-like figure lecturing on the subject and using a stuffed toy pig and chimpanzee to demonstrate how the two would "do it."

McCarthy was dismayed, but not really surprised, by some of the vicious personal attacks from certain fellow scientists. "I thought that *challenge* was the whole purpose of proposing a new theory, a new hypothesis," he says. But the blowback hasn't really fazed him: "Everywhere I look now, I see pig. And if you listen to me too much, it will happen to you too."

McCarthy's home turf is the city of Athens, Georgia — green on the banks of the Oconee River. It is a place that conjures two American idylls. One, the New Athens, looks pretty 21st century: suburbs, foodies, mixologists, tattooed and indecently clad coeds (on a hot day), the University of Georgia and its huge genetics department and a place down the hill that serves "some awesome tacos!" Three years ago some 4,000 denizens of this New Athens wrote in Charles Darwin for a congressional race.

Closer in, and underneath everything, percolates the Old Athens: unapologetically expansive front lawns, cigarettes, statues to fallen Confederates, beer joints that serve just beer, an easygoing daily newspaper to read on an easygoing afternoon. In the same congressional race, the citizens of Old Athens reelected Tea Party–favorite Paul Broun, famed for his flaming antiscience vitriol: "All that stuff I was taught about evolution and embryology and the big bang theory, all that is lies straight from the pit of hell."

McCarthy has spent most of his life studying those "lies." He earned his PhD in evolutionary genetics in 2003 from the University of Georgia, but his thinking about evolution began some 20 years before, when he was running a small construction company in Athens. In fact, as he tells it, he'd first read Darwin when he was 15, at his bibliophile grandmother's knee.

McCarthy came back to Darwin in his 20s. Reading Chapter 8 of *On the Origin of Species* — "On Hybridism" — changed everything:

> It gave a lot of examples of fertile hybrids — and that struck me. Until then I was under the belief that all hybrids were sterile, like the mule. But Darwin was really saying fertility was not an on-or-off proposition. The hybrids produced from one type of cross can be much more fertile or viable than those from another.

McCarthy pauses, then gives in to a bit of understandable intellectual afterburn: "I can guess that either most scientists have read that and dismissed it, or they haven't really read Darwin at all."

McCarthy kept reading and thinking about hybrids. If hybrids from some crosses were fertile, couldn't new forms of life be produced in that way? If so, what about *Homo sapiens*? Ever since grammar school, when he first read about the discovery of Lascaux Cave, McCarthy had been interested in the question of human origins. Now, Darwin's chapter put that subject in a different light. Could we be hybrids? If so, who were our parents?

McCarthy learned about a method biologists commonly use to identify putative hybrids of unknown origin. So he decided to apply it to humans. Investigators first look for an organism that shares many traits with the suspected hybrid, and then pose it as one probable parent. (In the case of humans that would be the chimpanzee.) They then make a list of all the traits in the proposed hybrid that don't appear in that first parent. The animal with the greatest number of those traits would be the likely second parent.

"I wanted to find that other parent, to know what happened long ago out there in the forest," McCarthy says. He was looking for one of Buffon's hypothetical trysts, but a special one, the long lost dalliance that, among all the "illegitimate pleasures shared by creatures of separate species," led to the production of the human race.

McCarthy searched the literature to find all the traits that distinguished humans from chimps and bonobos. In the end he was able to find about 100, most of which experts said distinguished us not only from apes but also from all other primates. These traits, he discovered, are consistently found in pigs. Among the most compelling is the human kidney, which is of a type ("multipyramidal with a bean-shaped cortex") that occurs in no other known animal except the pig. Other traits we share with pigs — our bare skin, our thick layer of subcutaneous fat, the aberrant design of our skin's circulatory system — are not found in other primates, including our light-colored eyes and our protrusive rubbery nose.

Many of our piglike features, then, are externally visible. As McCarthy puts it, "Through my eyes, humans are pretty much just chimps in a pig skin."

But still — and McCarthy readily admits this — we have many more traits in common with chimpanzees than we do with pigs. So how does he reconcile this fact with the idea that we're pig-chimp hybrids? By assuming that we are the products of *repeated backcrossing* to chimpanzee.

Backcrossing falls under the heading of the various mechanisms that McCarthy dubs stabilization processes. It rapidly — in terms of geological time, instantaneously — produces a new type of organism (Gould's punctuation) with descendants that are stable in subsequent generations (Gould's stasis).

What is backcrossing? When you cross two parents and get a hybrid, that hybrid — if it's fertile — can mate either with another hybrid or with individuals of either of the two parental types. For example, a liger is produced when a tiger mates with a lion. The liger can be mated back ("backcrossed") to, say, a lion. Genetically, the resulting backcross hybrid would be only 1/4 tiger. If that backcross hybrid then backcrossed again to a lion, the result would be a hybrid that was only 1/8 tiger, and so forth. In such a scenario, one would soon only expect a few tiger traits to remain within an overall lion background.

In the same way, McCarthy says, with an initial cross between a pig and a chimp-like animal, with several generations of backcrossing to chimp, you could end up with a backcross hybrid that is mostly chimpanzee but with a significant percentage of piglike traits. Such are humans, he suspects.

The tryst that would permit this crossover of traits, McCarthy says, would likely require a pig father and a chimp mother. There are various facts that point to this conclusion, but mainly it's the fact that mammalian and avian hybrids produced in an initial cross are generally much more likely to backcross to the mother's "side of the family."

As McCarthy tells it, one moment brought the whole thesis together. It happened one day while he was reading a book about swine anatomy in the stacks of the science library at the University of Georgia. He came across a picture of pig vocal cords. Apes, he already knew, do not have cords. (They have a ridge made of cartilage.) The book in front of him showed that not only do pigs have vocal cords, but also that they have them in the *same form as humans*. "When I saw that, a chill ran up my spine," he says. "It was a watershed event for me. From then on, it was hard for me not to see pig shining through the chimp in human beings."

The idea that new types of organisms arise abruptly and then remain the same thereafter — then known as saltation — reigned before Darwin. Saltation let the era's freethinkers get away with heresy; it was a way to make divine origins politically compatible with the era's new scientific speculation about human origins. God starts things, God ends things. Yet even after Darwin's later intellectual triumphs, saltation remained a vivid scientific argument — one to which even the great 20th-century geneticist T. H. Morgan hewed before his work with mutating fruit fly genes sent him back to Darwin and natural selection.

But later on in the 20th century, evolutionary thinking grew increasingly monochromatic. In the 1930s, what became known as the Modern Synthesis congealed into a powerful scientific narrative. Among its central tenets was the concept of reproductive isolation: that new species can only be formed and maintained if they create a *barrier* to hybridization. Introducing the notion of successful fertile hybrids — the kind McCarthy proposes — into that theory is to throw a bomb into the establishment formula. It was not at all, McCarthy says, a welcome idea.

Modern Synthesis eventually became the standard against which all other theories of human evolution competed. In the 1940s, such thinkers as Julian Huxley — the grandson of Thomas Huxley, one of Darwin's greatest defenders — and Theodosius Dobzhansky — the brilliant Ukrainian fruit fly geneticist — rendered the Synthesis into an even more compelling, if inflexible, doctrine. Social anxieties figured heavily, in McCarthy's view. Periodic waves of creationism — and the need to respond to it — forged what he sees as a kind of religion of its own, science's default rejoinder to the nuts.

Inside the academy, the Synthesis forged a prickly and closed discipline. Important careers were built on it, true, but there were also epic lost opportunities. The Nobel Laureate Barbara McClintock, who in the 1940s discovered the so-called jumping genes — transposons — now familiar to any college biology major, was ostracized for so long that, as she later noted, "I just stopped publishing in 1953." (She began again in the 1980s.) Though his punctuated equilibrium was widely embraced by his fellow paleontologists, Gould drew fire from geneticists, who continued to hew to the Synthesis. And proponents of epigenetics — the study of heritable trait changes *not* brought about by changes in DNA — were long marginalized despite growing evidence, because their claims didn't fit with accepted theory — for example their suggestions that acquired traits can be inherited. Now epigenetics is a driving force in mainstream genetics, and an ATM for NIH funding.

The Modern Synthesis ran particularly deep in the burgeoning genetics department of the University of Georgia. One of McCarthy's advisors, Wyatt Anderson, a National Academy member, came right out of the Dobzhansky lab. McCarthy spent a few years in Anderson's lab during the early '90s, a period during which Anderson served as dean of the University of Georgia's College of Arts and Sciences.

"Wyatt was very conservative in his approach to science," says McCarthy. As such, he seemed to have little interest in hybridization. "But he respected me as a scholar, which I think is the reason he generously offered me a place in his lab, despite his apprehensive attitude toward my work."

The fact that McCarthy wasn't directly working on Anderson's projects meant that he had to earn his keep teaching biology and genetics, and as the departmental computer consultant. (He'd been an undergraduate math major.) Because he helped them with numbers, most people in the department put up with McCarthy's off-the-grid ideas about hybrids.

There were so many questions to be answered! How common was hybridization in a natural setting? How many crosses produced fertile hybrids? How many different kinds of stabilization processes were there? It began to look as if genetics *could* explain Gould's observed fact.

For centuries it has been widely believed, even by many scientists, that hybridization between animals occurs only in captivity — zoo animals penned together and forced to mate, birds trapped in a cage without access to a mate of their own kind. But the idea that hybrids needed humans to help the process along did not square with McCarthy's encyclopedic knowledge of bird hybrids — he'd documented more than 4,000 different types of crosses, about half occurring in a natural setting. And they were overwhelmingly fertile: for every avian cross that produced sterile hybrids, he'd found seven where the hybrids had managed to have offspring. He began researching a new list — compiling the thousands of available reports about hybrid mammals. And, as it turned out, fecund hybrids seemed to be about as common among mammals as they had been among birds. "I kind of saw myself as a journalist — I simply wanted to report as many detailed cases as I could find, and then let the reader decide."

McCarthy's pig-chimp thesis pushes hybridization one problematic step further. After all, he's not proposing a mating between two closely related species; he's talking about matings between two very distinct types of organisms. Conventional wisdom has long held that such distant crosses are impossible. "That's the most important issue for Gene's pig-chimp thing," says David Geiser, who was a graduate student in the genetics department at UGA with McCarthy. "The distance between the pig and the chimp is huge."

But "distance" may not be the impregnable barrier it's said to be. Two of the most commonly cited barriers of this type are the differences in the parents' chromosome counts and the lengths of their gestation periods. According to the 20th century's foremost authority on mammalian hybrids, Annie P. Gray, there is "no close correlation [...] between the chromosome count or the duration of gestation and the ability of species to hybridize."

After all, what does distance really mean? McCarthy points out that it is well established that chickens and turkeys can hybridize. And yet, most people would agree that they are very "distinct" types of animals.

"After looking at so many different crosses," he says,

> the evidence on hybridization taken as a whole suggests there is some sort of unrecognized mechanism that allows a small percentage of hybrids from some of these distant crosses to develop and mature. The result is the production of occasional very rare hybrids that are very weird.

On his website, McCarthy quotes reports about a wide variety of bizarre hybrids, including dog × cow, chicken × duck, and even rabbit × pigeon. When asked whether he took such reports seriously, he replies,

> I neither believe them nor disbelieve them. I simply report that they exist and quote them. In fact, I don't think belief has any place in science. Belief is the stuff of religion. Within a scientific context, I make every effort never to believe *anything* that I don't absolutely have to believe.

There are animals that give even mainstream biologists pause. The platypus, *Ornithorhynchus anatinus*, has the bill of a duck, but the rest of its body, except for its webbed feet, is like a beaver's. It spends most of its time in the water and is one of the very few egg-laying mammals. When 18th-century explorers sent home a sketch and a pelt of the beast, many regarded it as an elaborate hoax by some bonkers taxidermist. Even after researchers documented its existence, no one could quite agree what it was: Mammal? Bird? Reptile? Modern genomics vexed the subject even more. The platypus has 10 sex chromosomes — some like those of mammals, some like those birds. In 2008, *Nature* published a draft of the animal's genome, revealing the presence of two genes that previously were observed only in birds, amphibians, and fish — but not in mammals.

Such findings do not — or should not — go entirely against expectation, McCarthy wrote me in one of his precise yet playful emails. "After all, it's not as if a mammal spermatozoon that suddenly found itself in the cloaca of a bird would clasp its blushing cheeks and cry, 'Oh my ears and whiskers! I should *not* be here! *Whatever* shall I do?'"

McCarthy's ideas made him a target, and it was not just an intellectual debate. "It was a source of mocking in the department — and often by not the most well-read people," says Geiser, now a professor of plant pathology at Penn State. "It was personal. Gene was hurt."

It did not help that McCarthy, despite his gentle demeanor — he doesn't use the "f-word" — could also breathe fire on the subject of careerism. "He was the so-called 'kook,'" says Susanne Warrenfeltz, a friend who was in the department at the time and who is now a research scientist at UGA. "He was always talking about pure science versus career science." In the realm of today's professionalized science, it did not endear.

The real problem was his sidelining of Darwin. "One thing evolutionists really, *really* want to believe in is Darwin," says Warrenfeltz. "They are so glad that they beat out God as the creator! So when Gene started talking about hybrids — even as the data grew — they did not want to hear it. It bothered them."

In 2006, McCarthy left the department, he says, "because I was tired of working for weenie PIs [principal investigators]." Like so many who get *pushed* out of a career, he wrote a novel — *The Department* — in which he let the bile flow, with recognizable portrayals of the tyrannical and immoral "weenies" he had to endure.

McCarthy didn't leave university life before gaining some converts. While at UGA, he spent several years in the lab of genetics professor John McDonald, now associate dean for biology at Georgia Tech. McDonald was sympathetic if not to the pig-chimp thesis itself then to his bigger ideas. He eventually gave McCarthy a research position. "He was a great researcher, and very enterprising with new ideas that you could actually test," says McDonald of McCarthy. "And you can imagine how that rubbed some people. Gene is simply insisting that the role of traditional speciation in human evolution be tested. He liked to push the limits. I like that. Others really don't.

"And I have to admit it, the more he talked about the pig-chimp thesis, the harder it was for me to look in the mirror and not see pig."

Growing up in Augusta, Georgia, a river town on the South Carolina border, McCarthy spent many of his childhood evenings talking with his invalid grandmother. A longtime participant in the Great Books Foundation discussion groups, she had him sit and read aloud to her many of her favorites, things a teenager would otherwise be unlikely to encounter, including Plutarch, Locke, most of Shakespeare — and Darwin.

As he got older, he rebelled. There was discord at home, according to his friend and UGA colleague Stuart Katz: "His father kicked him out of the house." McCarthy, who was 16 at the time, left high school and took off hitchhiking across the US, doing manual labor, often camping out, and even spending some nights under bridges.

But something happened out there in the forest. When McCarthy came back from his adventures, he was — as all parents of rebel children hope they become — "motivated." He had discovered something — strength, perhaps some toughness. Now 20, he headed back to school, got his BS in math and a Phi Beta Kappa key, and eventually entered graduate school. He came across as resourceful, independent. The independence came with an edge. "If he thinks you are not telling the truth," says Katz, "he's pretty much done with you." Not exactly a trait for professional success. McCarthy and his ideas were largely ignored.

But what the old world of science and scientific publishing cannot countenance, the new world of electronic media and scientific entrepreneurism can — and does. In 2008, he says, after Oxford backpedaled on their offer to publish a tome presenting his alternative theory of evolution (it was under contract for nearly a year), McCarthy decided to publish it on his website, *Macroevolution.net*, rather than go through another protracted submission process. He got buy-in from advertisers and, according to McCarthy, many supporters.

These days he's spending a lot of time using a new computer program that he created to look for traces of pig genes in the human genome. He calls it BoomStick, after the nickname for a sawed-off shotgun. It takes at random millions of short pieces of the pig genome (the "pellets" of the shotgun blast) and finds their matches, if any, in the target human genome. The result is a picture of each chromosome in the target genome showing where pig matches concentrate. The algorithm is computationally intensive; things are going very slowly, especially since McCarthy doesn't have access to adequate computer facilities. "We've got a long way to go," he says.

> The human genome is so vast. And who knows exactly what we're looking for? The problem with backcrossing is that it so dilutes the genetic contribution from the non-backcross parent — which in this case would be that from the pig — that it becomes hard to recognize. So it's like looking for what may or may not be a needle in 400 haystacks.

Today, McCarthy's most influential supporter is John Avise, also a former UGA professor. Now a professor at UC Irvine, Avise is one of the world's leading thinkers on evolutionary genetics, which he's explored through his work on fish, birds, mollusks, rodents, turtles, and a number of other organisms.

Avise is interested in McCarthy's network model of evolution, which pictures evolutionary descent not as a tree of life but as a web — with all of the various types of organisms that stabilization processes produce interconnected by hybridization. Citing McCarthy in his recent book, *In the Light of Evolution*, Avise notes:

> If the network model [...] proves to be more nearly correct for many taxonomic groups, then the challenges for [...] evolutionary biology will be entirely different (McCarthy, 2008). First, phylogeneticists would have to admit that their dream of reconstructing a branched tree of life had been merely a pipedream [...]. Traditional concepts of species, phylogeny, ancestry, and classification, as well as the significance of reproductive isolation, would all have to be reevaluated.

Biologists would have to embrace the notion that biological processes falling somewhat outside the standard neo-Darwinian paradigm [...] could play major and previously underappreciated roles in evolution. They would have to reevaluate the origins of genetic variation.

"I see Gene as potentially an outstanding scientific entrepreneur," Avise says. "He's got the tools — he's dogged, independent, and a very good writer.

"He just hasn't sold himself."

THE GARDEN PARTY

FREDERIC TUTEN

"WHAT I LIKE MOST in art is disquietude," I said, my hand reaching for the martini pitcher.

"Expatiate on this later, after the party. Or maybe never," Alice said. "And please get dressed."

We were in the garden, by the pool, the patio umbrella casting a bronze shadow over me in the milky sun.

"I'm dressed."

"Pajamas is not what I had in mind," she said, slyly moving the pitcher out of my reach.

Behind me, a white two-story house, mine and hers. Similar houses of varying size and manifest affluence stretched in line row after row to a vanishing point. A flower garden in luxuriant bloom — our gardener sees to that. A kidney-shaped pool, where a giant orange rabbit spins slowly in a delicate breeze.

"And get rid of the rabbit. It's not funny."

"It's meant to hit a disquieting note, a discordant tone, like the unexpected that I love in art, as I mentioned a moment ago."

"Yes, and as you have mentioned for a decade. You should never have a martini before guests arrive. Or maybe ever. It brings out the pontifical in you."

"I'm not in the mood for a party. Phone everyone and say I'm sick. Chills and cough and shakes. A whiff of the plague."

I was happy sitting with my view of Main Street in the near distance, and beyond that the shopping mall on a hill, and beyond that a highway, choked with cars and trucks, bordered by a forest of young trees gasping for air.

"You call," Alice said.

"Then who's going to believe I'm sick? Who's coming anyway?"

"The usual. Mary Holiday and her husband, the doctor; the bankers, Jesse and his brother Frank; Eric Armstrong and his fiancée, Honey Flakes McBride, the former golf pro that you flirt with; Charles Coverdale, the creep who sold you the fake Rolex. Then there's the indicted mortgage broker, George le Blanc, and the defrocked missionary, Padre Paul."

"That's it?"

"Not at all. The mayor and the sheriff; the high school principal and his wife, the town slut; the retired army private, our assemblyman, and everyone from my firm who matters."

A deer, followed by a bear, a fox, a raccoon, and a bobcat, took their time strolling before us. The bear turned and, in the most cavalier, affronting way, tossed a shredded bag of pretzels into the pool. I quickly got distracted. "Do you smell smoke," I asked, rising from my chaise lounge.

"Of course! Just turn your head. Jack and Jan's house is on fire."

"Again?"

Fire engines drew up with sirens and horns blasting. Firemen dragged hoses, quivering like flattened pythons, into the garden, and milled before the burning house. They chattered, smoked cigarettes, played cards, and shot dice while Jack and Jan stood by, studying the fire. I waved and they waved back, smiling.

"Do you think the fire will spread to us?" Alice asked.

"Not a chance," I said. "Unless the wind blows this way."

The Fire Chief called over the fence. "Do you mind if we pail some water from your pool?"

"Be my guest," I said. "Be our guest," Alice added.

"Thanks for the *aqua*, our pool's kaput," Jan said, coming to visit.

"Don't forget to come by later," Alice said. "It's just us and the old gang."

"And invite anyone you like," I said. "By the way, your porch is ablaze."

"And they claim it's fire resistant!" Jack said.

"It's just cheap pressed wood. I told you so," Jan said, breathing out a plume of smoke. "My husband's always looking for bargains," she added, turning to the Fire Chief and the six handsome young firemen carrying metal pails.

"Please don't throw your cigarettes in the pool," my wife asked the firemen, in what I thought was a seductive voice.

"Let's get started, boys," the Chief said. The men lined up, filled their pails, and, in a file, took turns splashing water on the burning house.

"The fire's traveling to your second floor," Alice said.

"It's a crisp and orderly fire," I added.

"Yes, it's a fire with precision, which I prefer to the chaos of the fireplace," Jan said, looking exceptionally youthful.

"So few people appreciate nuance," my wife said. "That's why we cherish you as neighbors."

"I was saying to Alice just before you came how much I like the discordant in art."

"I couldn't agree more," Jan said. "Art must be discordant or be nothing at all."

"But not stridently or flamboyantly so, as with Surrealism, and its obvious and conventional gimmicks," Jack added.

"I agree wholly, Jack. And quietude must underline and foil the discord," I said, pleased with myself.

Just then my wife, shielding her eyes from the blaze, said: "Don't your in-laws live in the second story?"

"Why, yes, what a good memory you have," Jack said.

"But those two are never going to leave," Jan noted. "Once they're glued to their game shows they stay put, earthquake or tornado or fire, no matter what."

"In my younger days, I used to like *Wheel of Fortune*," the Fire Chief said. "There was also one with different doors, some had prizes behind them and you had to guess which door."

"Why don't you come by later for drinks and the barbecue?" Alice told the Fire Chief. "And the boys too, of course."

"Love to, but there's a giant conflagration on the other side of town that needs attending to."

"Do you have enough pails, Chief?" Jan asked. "We have a few in the garage we can lend you."

"The problem's not the pails. It's the pools. They have almost no pools over in that section of town."

"How some people live!" Jan exclaimed. "I myself value a pool above a kitchen. After all, there's always takeout. But I suppose not everyone feels that way."

I wanted to tell them about a painting in line with what we had been discussing earlier. But then Jan said, "It's getting really warm out here, may we have something to drink."

I was appalled by my lack of hospitality and rattled the ice cubes in the shaker. With my apologies, I made a new batch of martinis and poured all around. Within a few minutes, Jack said, "This is great, Ted. Even minus the olives, you make a perfect martini."

A whine, whizzing and a popping overhead, red, white, and blue flares burst in the sky. A parade of cars, trucks, floats with banners of the American Legion, the Elks, the Veterans of Foreign Wars, White's Pharmacy flowed along Main Street, followed by a marching band blasting John Philip Sousa.

"What is it anyway, the Fourth or Memorial Day or Thanksgiving?" Jack asked, waving away the smoke veiling the air about us.

"It's one of those days," Jan said, her hair frizzing in the fire's heat. "Anyway, it's getting too hot here, mind if we go over and sit in your pool?"

"That's a good idea," Alice said, "let's all go." But at that moment, a van arrived, crushing the flower beds and indenting the grass. "Oh! Finally," Alice cried, "I thought they'd never show."

The caterers quickly set up 10 round tables and chairs and umbrellas and two wet bars.

"Where's the food?" Alice asked, in a modulated panic.

Another van skidded to a stop; the driver emerged waving a paper. Four men in aprons hauled out and spread out on the grass: five gutted pigs, six sides of beef, five 50-pound plastic bags of chopped meat, eight plucked chickens, headless but alive.

"Sign the receipt," the driver said.

"What about the buns and the condiments?"

"What about the beverages?" I called out.

"The delivery truck's overturned on Utopia Avenue, and now it's a river of sodas and booze," the driver said.

"Where," Alice asked, "are the bartenders and the wait staff? They're already late!"

"Twelve have Ebola, and two have gone to the fireworks. Sign," the driver said, thrusting the pen toward Alice's face.

"Not in this lifetime."

The driver nodded to the four men, who, shouldering the bags of meat, made their way to the pool.

"Give me the pen," Alice said, "but forget the tip."

"We better get going," the Chief said, pointing to the smoke-choked sky. "Before we know it, the whole town will go up."

"Can we come with you?" Jan and Jack called out, sunk to their necks in the pool.

"Why not, I know how you kids love a fire."

"Come back soon," I shouted, waving to the departing fire truck, its sirens overriding my voice.

"I'm so glad they left," I said. "There's no serious conversation in them, nothing beyond a few minutes. I was about to talk about an old master painting I love, a man walking in a serene landscape and quiet sky. You couldn't ask for a nicer day. But when you look up close, you see a giant snake waiting, unseen in the man's path."

"Have you noticed," Alice asked, before I could continue, "that our house has caught fire?"

"Our neighbors' houses as well," I said, pointing out the obvious. House after house burning in succession, like a row of falling dominoes. Sparrows dropped from the sky like charred rocks.

"What's the point of ever making plans?" Alice said, glumly.

Elegy with Roots

BIANCA STONE

I was surrounded by taxidermy
with my semiautomatic pistol
antique, through gunpowder
the Coke cans of grief emptied
10 billion million stars
the eucalyptus sprig
airborne
so many stones
when you take up the ground
they throw themselves in a pile
the hole filled
with a certain sea
the human brain shifts
like an orangutan learning
to open locked doors and drink beer –

this is the loneliest sport in the world
jellyfish wrapped
around your arm –
I don't want to relish the beauty of holiness
or reflect the divine universe – know,
I said to the hole we put her in –
roots hung
from the ash tree
we threw the grasses in
the loam in
and I went in –

up through the fissures
the livid perfume of the body came and spun like a top
before cooling into sheets of rock ⁄⁄

REBECCA FARR
BRIDGE, 2013
MIXED MEDIA ON WOOD
48 X 36"
COURTESY OF THE ARTIST AND KLOWDEN MANN GALLERY
PHOTO BY LEE THOMPSON

BIANCA STONE

Epitaph in Reverse

BIANCA STONE

It feels like a town square slowly deserted.
But it's like a forest falling in the forest
and all the crippled that gather
around it to mourn,
they feel like righteous holy wars.
You're very near me now.
With your purse full and zipped.
You're in a dirigible
and hovering over the Great Lakes.
I listen at the phone
because doom comes
whenever it feels like it. Or can come
slow, drawn out over many months.

We come to life and our life
is a 10-foot statue of our mother
and our mother's mother.
I saw someone, frozen out there
her face covered in birds,
her arms perpetually up in her hair
I saw the endless procession
of anorexic stars
spread their fingers across the sky
in five thin paths
each leading to a different version
of heaven. I saw the house shudder and shake,
stand up on two chicken feet
and walk away over the mountain.
And everyone saw the gravedigger,
that shy man in boots
from down the road
standing with his hat in his hands
beside the backhoe -
you were called back by a secretary
in reckless abandonment.
Called back by a secretary without her glasses on,
with her vengeance pouring from its crate.
Called back tired of waiting. Or
not called back at all … but left here,
right over there
in that spot behind the barn
that is farthest from the brook.

TIPPING POINT

DEB DURHAM

THE SOUND IS relentless, like a buoy bell at sea, pulling me through the comfortable torpor of pouring rain, churning waves, and night sky. I would prefer to stay here, floating without responsibility, but the sound yanks me out of sleep and back into my body. My right hip feels as though a railroad spike has been driven through it. I sit up, rubbing my eyes, trying to focus.

It is my grandfather's voice that has dragged me into consciousness: "Debbie, I think she's dead! Is she dead? I think she's dead!" The hospital blanket falls around my ankles and nearly trips me as I stand. I stumble over to the bed where my grandmother lies, mouth open, eyes closed. Her face looks like candle wax just before it begins to melt, and I say the first thing that pops into my sleep-deprived head, "Oh my God, she is so dead."

It's around five a.m. My grandmother, at the end of a yearlong battle with lung cancer, has been in this room for almost two weeks. A month earlier she'd been told she was cancer-free; but a persistent ache took her back to the doctors, and the news that she had very little time. She's in the hospice wing in the hospital where I was born — I am the only member of this family, immediate or extended, who lives outside Bloomington, Indiana, a university town where my family settled seven generations ago. My family is wholly town; their only relation to gown is through employment as security guards and janitors.

My father had called me in Chicago, my home for the last 12 years. When I heard his voice on the phone I felt a vapory tendril of fear, like fog, under my rib cage.

"Your grandma's in the hospital," he said.

And this was alarming. It's not only that my father hardly ever calls; my grandmother has always been a firm believer in not bothering others with her health problems. Usually I don't hear about any illness until months after the fact.

"Should I come down?" I asked.

"If you want to."

"Does Grandma want me to?"

"Yes."

I wanted to yell at my father for being a dumbass except I didn't know him well enough to get that personal. Instead I called Southwest and booked my flight. The next day I walked into the hospital room full of relatives. Somebody said, "Here she is, Norma." As the first grandchild and the only girl out of six I had always been the clear favorite.

"I'm so happy you're here," she told me, tiredly squeezing my hand.

"Grandma, where else would I be?"

She seemed to be doing well and enjoying her company. But my grandfather looked exhausted, and his sister Sue whispered to me that he hadn't eaten or been home in two days. When my grandmother drifted off to sleep I told my granddad that I was starving and asked him if he would buy me lunch in the cafeteria. He was glad to have a person who needed something he could give. We ate meatloaf and mashed potatoes and red Jell-O. I have always found hospital cafeterias comforting — a place to forget for a while — and the food tasted good to me.

After lunch my grandfather took me back to the house to rest, and fell asleep, himself, while I was napping. It was evening when we got back to the hospital to find my father, alone, sitting in a chair on one side of the bed and watching my grandmother breathe. He left soon after we arrived and thus began the pattern of our days.

We sat with her in shifts. I was on night duty, keeping vigil with my grandfather. My Aunt Gloria came to relieve us around seven every morning. My father took the early evenings, and his brother Mike and other family members — my Great-Aunts Mary and LaDonna and their children, Tareva or Tim or Kenny Lee — came on weekends and whenever else they could. I developed an insatiable hunger for the thick cinnamon-battered French toast in the cafeteria where my grandfather and I stopped every morning on the way home.

Nothing in a hospital room is soft. It's all sharp angles and hard washable surfaces. Everything must be easy to sterilize against possible infection: rubber tubing, molded plastic, vinyl and chrome, tile-covered concrete. Illness requires sanitary conditions, even the terminal kind. My grandmother's deterioration began almost immediately after my arrival. Despite knowing the end of the story it was shocking to witness.

Lucidity abruptly departed as her morphine dosage climbed. I watched her play a game of euchre with imaginary friends. I fought to stifle teary giggles. The skin behind her ears was raw from the elastic strap of her oxygen mask, and my grandfather made padding from layers of Kleenex. Her lips were peeling from the oxygen that she couldn't be without. My heartache was a physical pain that radiated to my fingertips. They throbbed in rhythm with my pulse.

Cooler air made it easier for my grandmother to breathe, and the room grew so cold that I took to wearing one of her old-lady cardigans and stealing blankets off hospital supply carts to stay warm during the night. Half of the room was in cave-like darkness; in the other half, fluorescent lighting abraded the eyes. The plastic arm of the chair that I dozed in tortured my back — but it was the most comfortable seat in the room. The chill, the lack of sleep, and the burning in my stomach from bad hospital coffee gave the nights the charged clarity of an acid trip.

My grandfather seemed unaware of the increasingly frigid temperature in the room, or what that implied. For 30 minutes at a time, he knelt on the tiled concrete, massaging warmth into his wife's hands and feet. I wanted to help him, to take my turn, but it seemed such an intimate turf war, this battle between my grandfather and death — my very presence felt like a violation. Their 60th wedding anniversary was just weeks away.

My grandparents met in 1943, when they were 16 and 18, at Cascades Park, a half-mile away from where they live now. I asked them once what first attracted them to each other. My grandfather said that it was the fact that my grandmother was the youngest in her family and had no brothers and sisters to mind like the last girl he went with. My grandmother said it was because he made her laugh. In pictures they are a rosy-cheeked and pompadoured cliché — they are breathtaking. The only time they were ever apart is when he was in the Air Force during World War II. My grandfather has told me the story of how he went AWOL and hitchhiked from New York City to Indiana with five dollars in his pocket so that he could see her and their two babies before he shipped out to Portugal. She told me that she had a dream once that he'd come home — a dream so vivid that she jumped out of bed and opened the door to find only moonlight and an empty gravel road.

They shared the loss of a child, Ricky, the baby of the family. He was accidentally shot by a careless neighbor when he was four. My grandfather once said that when he was told the news he heard something like music in his head and that he never went to church again.

Watching my grandmother's body literally withdraw from life, listening to her rattling breaths and her drug-induced ramblings, I've learned that there is a tipping point for life itself: at some juncture the body can't come back. It must go forward into death. It's in this cold hard room that I've learned the guilty tedium of waiting for a person to die.

I run for a nurse so that someone official is in the room. There's nothing she can do — except confirm for my grandfather that there is nothing that she can do. He needs this. And even so he continues to stand there, looking at his wife, as if he can't quite understand what has happened. I telephone my father to tell him that his mother is dead, and make sure that my aunt and uncle will be informed. Back in the room, I tell my grandfather that his children are on the way. He comes to himself a bit, and says something about letting the rest of the family know. After all of the waiting, there is business to attend to — time for me to head back to the house and start making calls.

I have never been an integral part of my father's family. My parents divorced when I was five, and my mother, a devout Jehovah's Witness, limited my contact with his relations. She has never approved of their tavern-going, profanity-loving, thoroughly secular ways.

As an adult, I managed to become close to my grandparents — closer to them than to my father — but I only know the rest by name. I reveal few details of my life to them. I don't want to take the chance. My world is theater, Sunday brunch, and fair-trade coffee. Theirs is deer hunting, fishing, and fried anything. It's not that I see my own ways as superior; it's just that I'm protective of my choices. I don't care to view my thespian friends, my artist friends, my queer friends, and my own burgeoning queerness through their lens.

But when my grandmother went into the hospital for her last stay, I was the only person who could coax my grandfather from her side to eat and sleep. Family members came to *me* to consult about what he might need. And now I am stepping into a role of even greater responsibility: it's up to me to begin to arrange for the rites and rituals surrounding the celebration and mourning of my grandmother's life and death.

It is May — but I had forgotten about spring in that icy room. Walking out of the hospital and down the zigzagging flights to the parking lot at the bottom of the hill, I step out of shadow into lemony sunlight. It is a perfect spring morning of a sort particular to southern Indiana. The sky is watercolor cerulean, dappled with cottony wisps of cloud. There is a breeze, soft but solid, against my skin. It's like a rose petal massage, cool and velvety, rubbing life back into my arms and face. Crossing the lot, I breathe deeply, my head filled with the perfumes of lilac and dogwood. I drive back to the house with the windows down. Flowering trees and bushes line the street: more lilac and dogwood — redbud, forsythia, and crab apple. They frame the restored Sears & Roebuck bungalows and absorb the traffic sounds from the town square three blocks away. I cruise through this flowery hush, stopping at the local food co-op to buy a coffee (fair-trade) and an apricot scone. Holding these tokens of my life as I live it in Chicago restores me a little.

This little green house. My grandparents lived here together for the entire 60 years of their marriage. My grandfather grew up in the little blue house next door; my family has owned this land since 1919. I remember the apple orchard that used to abut the property. I remember the Friday evenings I spent here as a child (from 5:00 to 9:00 in the evening exactly — that was the extent of my father's visitation rights) watching television and celebrating the holidays that were forbidden at my mother's. I remember all the visits from Chicago, sitting at the kitchen table with Grandma and Granddad, eating homemade pie and listening to stories of their hardscrabble life. My grandmother was the family's master pie maker. My grandfather was — still is — the family's legendary pie lover. During the last year, she'd used her good days to make piecrusts. There are stacks of them stored in the freezer downstairs.

I sit with my coffee on the prickly lawn, and I remember. I stare down the hill behind my grandparents' house at the remnants of the concrete picnic table, grown over now with blackberry bushes, and I remember. I see the buckle in the earth halfway to the bottom that threw me off of my tricycle when I was three. I rub the scar that is still visible on my right knee, and I remember.

Picking myself up off the grass, I go inside and grab the cordless phone, my grandmother's address book, and a glass of iced tea. I settle myself on the back porch where the sun beats hot and alive on my head and shoulders. The birds sing their particular songs of birdie seduction. One of the squirrels my grandparents have taught to come to the door for peanuts and grapes starts tentatively up the back steps; I click my tongue and toss him the rest of my scone. I will miss my grandmother — I'll miss the way she loved me as though I were still a child. Holding the book open in my lap, squinting to read her spidery hand, I take a breath and start dialing.

Without her I am older.

MARY KAY ZURAVLEFF is the author of three novels. Her latest, *Man Alive!*, was named a *Washington Post* 2013 Notable Book. She is the recipient of a 2015 DC Commission on the Arts Fellowship and is currently working on a book inspired by her Russian Orthodox ancestors.

GAVIN TOMSON'S writing has appeared in the *Los Angeles Review of Books*, *Salon*, *Double Dot*, *The Awl*, *Full Stop*, *The Puritan*, and *The Dalhousie Review*. He's the winner of *The Dalhousie Review*'s inaugural short story contest, and he lives in Toronto, where he's at work on his first collection of short stories. You can follow him @GavinTomson.

GREG GLAZNER'S books of poetry are *From the Iron Chair*, which won the Walt Whitman Award, and *Singularity*. Excerpts from his recently completed novel, *Opening the World*, have appeared in *Poetry*, *The Idaho Review*, *Blackbird*, and other magazines. His collaboration with composer Garrett Shatzer, *At the Blinds*, premiered at San Francisco's Center for New Music in November 2014. He teaches at UC Davis and in the low-residency MFA program at Pacific Lutheran University.

JEAN VALENTINE is the author of 12 books of poetry, most recently *Break the Glass*. She has lived and taught most of her life in New York City.

Translator bio: **CURTIS BAUER** is the author of two poetry collections, most recently *The Real Cause for Your Absence* (C&R Press, 2013). He is also a translator of poetry and prose from the Spanish; his publications include the full-length poetry collections *Eros Is More*, by Juan Antonio González Iglesias (Alice James Books, 2014) and *From Behind What Landscape*, by Luis Muñoz (forthcoming from Vaso Roto Ediciones in 2015). He is the publisher and editor of Q Avenue Press Chapbooks, the Spanish Translations Editor for From the Fishouse, and "Emerging Spanish Poets" Series Editor for Vaso Roto Ediciones. He teaches Creative Writing and Comparative Literature at Texas Tech University in Lubbock, Texas.

STEVEN BELLETTO is associate professor of English at Lafayette College. His most recent book is *No Accident, Comrade*.

BRÍAN HANRAHAN teaches and writes on media and film history. He lives in California.

ROLF POTTS is the author of two travel books, *Vagabonding* and *Marco Polo Didn't Go There*.

MAX RITVO is a poet living in Manhattan. He is a Poetry Society of America 2014 Chapbook Fellow for the chapbook *AEONS*. His poetry has also appeared or is forthcoming in the *Boston Review*, *The Best American Poetry* blog, and as a Poem-a-Day for poets.org. He is an assistant editor at *Parnassus: Poetry in Review* and a teaching fellow at Columbia.

CLARISSA TOSSIN received an M.F.A. from the California Institute of the Arts in 2009 and was a Core Fellow at the Museum of Fine Arts Houston from 2010 to 2012. Her recent solo exhibitions include *Streamlined: Belterra, Amazônia / Alberta, Michigan* at Museum of Latin American Art, Long Beach (2015); *How does it travel?* at Samuel Freeman, Los Angeles (2015); and *Transplanted (VW Brasilia)* at Galeria Luisa Strina, São Paulo (2014). She lives and works in Los Angeles.

LOUISE STEINMAN is the author of *The Crooked Mirror: A Memoir of Polish-Jewish Reconciliation* (Beacon Press, 2013). She curates the ALOUD series for the Library Foundation of Los Angeles and is co-director of the Los Angeles Institute for the Humanities at USC. She is the author of the award-winning memoir *The Souvenir: A Daughter Discovers Her Father's War.*

ALISSA WILKINSON is an assistant professor of English and humanities at The King's College in New York City. Her writing on culture, art, religion, and politics regularly appears in a wide range of publications including *The Washington Post*, *The Atlantic*, *Pacific Standard*, *Books & Culture*, *Movie Mezzanine*, *Christianity Today*, and others. She lives in Brooklyn.

JOHN STINTZI is a poet, potential novelist, book reviewer, visual artist, and Winnipeg expatriate currently working on his MFA in Creative Writing at Stony Brook University in Southampton, New York. His work can be found in *The Southampton Review*, *filling Station*, *CV2*, *The Malahat Review*, *Geez*, and on *Lemon Hound.*

ASHLEY RINDSBERG is a writer and editor who lives in Tel Aviv. The author of a collection of short stories, he's currently completing his first novel.

ELIZABETH ARNOLD'S most recent book is *Life* (Flood Editions, 2014). Newer poems have appeared recently or are forthcoming in *American Literary Review*, *Eco-Theo*, and *Ploughshares*. Arnold is on the MFA faculty at the University of Maryland and lives in Hyattsville, Maryland.

LYNNE SHARON SCHWARTZ'S most recent book is the essay collection *This Is Where We Came In*. Her novels include *Disturbances in the Field*, *Leaving Brooklyn* (nominated for a PEN/Faulkner Award for Fiction), *The Writing on the Wall*, and others. She's also published story and poetry collections, essays, and translations from Italian. She teaches at the Bennington Writing Seminars and at Columbia University's School of the Arts.

BARRIE JEAN BORICH is the author of *Body Geographic*, winner of a Lambda Literary Award and an IPPY Gold Medal. Borich is an associate professor at DePaul University in Chicago where she edits Slag Glass City, a digital nonfiction journal of the urban essay arts, and she also serves as a faculty member at the Rainier Writing Workshop.

ISHION HUTCHINSON was born in Port Antonio, Jamaica. His poetry collection, *Far District: Poems* (2010), won the PEN/Joyce Osterweil Award. Other honors include a Whiting Writers' Award, the Glenna Luschei Award from *Prairie Schooner*, and the Academy of American Poets' Larry Levis Prize. He is an assistant professor of English at Cornell University.

JONATHAN ALEXANDER is Professor of English, Education, and Gender & Sexuality Studies at the University of California, Irvine. The author, co-author, or editor of 10 books, he writes frequently about media, sexuality, and literacy — often all at the same time.

HAFIZAH GETER is a South Carolina native currently living in Brooklyn, New York. She is a Cave Canem fellow and was a semifinalist for the 2010 "Discovery" / *Boston Review* Contest. A recipient of a 2012 Amy Award from Poets & Writers, a 2013 Blacksmith House Emerging Writer, and a finalist in the Fifth Annual *Narrative Magazine* Poetry Prize, she was also a 2014 Ruth Lilly Poetry Fellowship finalist. Her poems have appeared or are forthcoming in *RHINO*, *Columbia: A Journal of Literature and Art*, *Linebreak*, *Narrative Magazine*, *Gulf Coast*, and *Boston Review*, among others. She is a poetry editor at Phantom Books. Find more of her work at www.hafizahgeter.com.

GREG CRITSER is the author of *Fat Land: How Americans Became the Fattest People in the World* (2003), *Generation Rx: How Prescription Drugs Are Altering American Lives, Minds, and Bodies* (2005), and *Eternity Soup: Inside the Quest to End Aging* (2010). He lives in Pasadena, California.

FREDERIC TUTEN has written about art, literature, and film in several periodicals including *Artforum*, *The New York Times*, *Vogue*; was an actor in an Alain Resnais movie; taught with Paul Bowles in Morocco; co-wrote the cult classic *Possession*; and along the way, earned a PhD in literature, three Pushcart Prizes, and a Guggenheim Fellowship.

He is the author of five novels: *The Adventures of Mao on the Long March*; *Tintin in the New World*; *Tallien: A Brief Romance*; *Van Gogh's Bad Café*; *The Green Hour*; and a book of interrelated short stories: *Self Portraits: Fictions*.

BIANCA STONE is the author of the celebrated, debut poetry collection *Someone Else's Wedding Vows*, and the forthcoming hybrid book, *Poetry Comics from The Book of Hours*. She is also contributing artist and collaborator with Anne Carson on a special edition of *Antigonick*, from New Directions. She is co-founder and editor of Monk Books, and chairs The Ruth Stone Foundation for Poetry and the Arts, an organization based in Vermont and Brooklyn, NY.

DEB DURHAM is currently pursuing an MFA in Creative Writing, with a focus on creative nonfiction, at the University of California, Riverside. Deb grew up in the untamed cornfields of southern Indiana, where she developed a taste for blue eye shadow and black velvet Elvis paintings. Thankfully, those days are behind her. Her essays have appeared in *South Loop Review*, *Qreview*, and on WBEZ Chicago's *Eight Forty-Eight*. As a solo performance artist, she has appeared at Victory Gardens Theater, Links Hall, and at Columbia College's Gender Fusion. She is currently at work on a solo show entitled *The Sacred Cow's Petting Zoo*. Current obsessions include her Chihuahua Rockhudson, teen romance novels of the 1950s, and writing the perfect paragraph.

REBECCA FARR
FOG, 2013
MIXED MEDIA ON WOOD PANEL
48 X 36"
COURTESY OF THE ARTIST AND KLOWDEN MANN GALLERY
PHOTO BY LEE THOMPSON